Intervening for Literacy

Intervening for Literacy
The Joy of Reading to Young Children

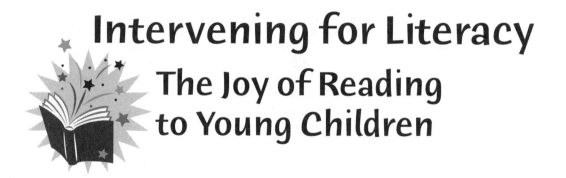

Charles Temple
Hobart and William Smith Colleges

James MaKinster
Hobart and William Smith Colleges

with

Jenna Logue

Lauren Buchmann

Gabriela Mrvova

Foreword by
Mark Gearan
President, Hobart and William Smith Colleges

PEARSON

Boston   New York   San Francisco
Mexico City   Montreal   Toronto   London   Madrid   Munich   Paris
Hong Kong   Singapore   Tokyo   Cape Town   Sydney

Senior Acquisitions Editor: Aurora Martínez Ramos
Series Editorial Assistant: Kevin Shannon
Senior Editorial-Production Administrator: Beth Houston
Editorial-Production Service: Kathy Smith
Senior Marketing Manager: Jennifer Armstrong
Composition and Prepress Buyer: Linda Cox
Manufacturing Buyer: Andrew Turso
Cover Administrator: Linda Knowles
Photo Research: Kathy Smith
Interior Design and Electronic Composition: Denise Hoffman

Cataloging-in-Publication data unavailable at press time.

ISBN 0-205-40277-1

Printed in the United States of America

10 9 8 7 6 5 4 3 2 1   08 07 06 05 04

Photo credits: p. 1, © Cindy Charles, PhotoEdit; pp. 25, 107, Nancy Sheehan
Photography; p 45, Lindfors Photography; pp. 71, 74, Lauren Buchmann;
p. 93, © Will Hart, PhotoEdit.

# Contents

c h a p t e r   f o u r
How Do We Help Language and Literacy Emerge?   71

chapter five
What Now?   107

 # Foreword

One of the many lessons I took from my tenure as Director of the Peace Corps was that the agency created in 1961 by President John F. Kennedy and brilliantly led by its first Director, Sargent Shriver, showed the power of an idea. At the end of the day, the concept of the Peace Corps was quite simple: send Americans to countries that need and want our help, they will share their skills, each culture will learn about the other and Americans will gain when the Volunteer "brings the world home" to share with them.

The power of an idea is also evident with Jumpstart and other efforts nationally to encourage volunteer service during college years. Many important service initiatives are happening each and every day on college campuses across the United States. From volunteer efforts in local elementary schools and food programs to important service learning courses integrated into the curriculum that allow for students' reflection of their volunteer experience—America's college students are making a difference.

Colleges and universities have an enormous opportunity to capture this volunteer spirit, and promote and enhance it in important curricular and co-curricular ways. Most students will only spend four Falls and four Springs as an undergraduate—a remarkably short period of time. As educators, we have a responsibility to ensure that students graduating into the twenty-first century have a full understanding of what citizenship must mean in this exciting time, and volunteer service must be part of that understanding.

As President of an institution that has a rich history of civic engagement and community service, I am proud of our students' initiative and faculty support for these priorities. It is no surprise, therefore, that two faculty colleagues have taken on this important research in this book with typical enthusiasm and dedication to service. Their work will be an important contribution as we advance our understanding of student engagement.

Mark D. Gearan
President
Hobart and William Smith Colleges

 # Preface

This book is written for you, the tens of thousands of good people who will be giving of your time to tutor young children. We admire you and we salute you, because helping a young person develop language and literacy is one of the most generous acts of service you can perform. Here's why.

If preschool children can get the kinds of playful and enjoyable experiences with books and print that an engaged parent—or an engaged tutor—can give them, those children will have an easier time of it when they learn to read later on. Knowing how to read will be a huge advantage to them, not only in school, where they must be able to read in order to learn their subjects, but later in adult life, when literacy will help them get and keep a fulfilling job, enable them to participate in civic life, and make them more alert to the world and to their own experiences. Just imagine making so much difference in a person's life. No wonder we say that tutoring a child in language and literacy is a generous thing for you to do.

Like a book we already read, a movie we already saw, we know in advance the stories of the children who probably won't learn to read and write adequately. A decade ago, we could tell by the time they reached the age of six which children were likely to fail, and why. Now research has pushed that age back to four, even three. We may be speaking here of the child you are about to tutor, a child you may not have met yet.

But if we know who is likely to fail, we know what kind of help that child will need. And that's where you come in. We can now say in fair detail what you can do in order to turn a child's trajectory toward success. But it will take hard work, patience, a generous heart, and informed judgment for you to make the difference you *can* make. This book is about the last of those. We assume you are bringing the rest.

The first three chapters of the book will tell you first who will have trouble in learning to read, and why that matters. Those chapters will also help you develop your own working theory of how children learn language and literacy (think of that as part of gaining "informed judgment"). The fourth chapter, a long and full one, will equip you with a "tool box" for helping grow children's language and literacy. And the fifth and final chapter will tell you what to do in case you decide you're pretty good at working with young people, and that you want to do more of this work.

Our institution, Hobart and William Smith Colleges, has long had an emphasis on service learning, and over the past twenty years, we have mounted programs through which college students volunteer to tutor children in reading. These are mostly not teacher education candidates—they are majors in psychology, public policy, sociology, pre-med, and even art or Greek. But after working with children for even a few sessions, they become fascinated and want to know more about how language and literacy development work. And each year more than a few of those students find a call to teach, and wonder what steps to take to move from volunteer to paid teacher. We have written this book for students like them: We're assuming you are a curious non-specialist, and that you might just decide to continue helping children learn.

In our experience, the most successful volunteer tutors don't try to go it alone: They work through well-organized programs. Hobart & William Smith Colleges started one of the first Student Literacy Corps projects in the late 1980s, which eventually morphed into America Reads when that program started in the early 1990s. America Reads is still going strong on our campus, and it features a fairly structured approach to teaching that we adopted from our good friend, Darrell Morris' Howard Street tutoring model (Morris, 1999).

A few years ago on our campus, we began a chapter of Jumpstart, a nationally organized tutoring project [http://www.jstart.org]. Jumpstart trains students on many college campuses throughout the United States to serve as tutors in language and literacy for children in Head Start and other early childhood education centers. On our campus, students rate Jumpstart highly for the training it gives them, plus the support when they are tutoring, and the esprit de corps with fellow Jumpstart volunteers both here and on other campuses. Jumpstart also provides guidance and opportunities to compete for scholarships for students who want to pursue their interest in teaching young children.

Most of the interviews with tutors and teachers that appear throughout this book were collected through our partners in the Jumpstart program. Jenna Logue, our Jumpstart project director, and Lauren Buchmann, a Jumpstart site leader at the time of this writing, both conducted interviews with people locally and nationally, and also took pictures for the project.

Jumpstart enjoys corporate sponsorship from American Eagle Outfitters, Starbucks, and Pearson. Jumpstart demonstrates a powerful model of support for community service, in which the service project becomes a vehicle of community outreach for sponsors from the business community, and engages not only their treasure, but their time and talents. This sort of relationship is a model worthy of attention from anyone interested in sustainable community development. As we will argue in this book, the challenge of helping all of our children become literate is so huge that it will require hefty investments of time, talent, and treasure from many quarters. In this effort, educators are finding valuable partners in the local and national business community.

The relationship between Jumpstart and the Pearson businesses (*The Financial Times*, Pearson Education, and The Penguin Group) is an enviable example of a productive, multi-faceted partnership between a non-profit organization and a corporation. With a multi-year $2.5 million commitment, Pearson teamed up with Jumpstart to create the Pearson Teacher Fellowship, a program designed to inspire talented university graduates to become preschool teachers in low-income communities. To date, Pearson has sponsored over 70 Pearson Teacher Fellows (see Chapter Five). In addition to the Fellowship Program, Pearson contributes in many other ways toward helping Jumpstart achieve its mission. They publish books for and inspired by Jumpstart, and send Jumpstart-affiliated schools learning materials for children. These include Pearson Early Learning's *Read Together Talk Together*, Penguin's *Only You* by award-winning author Rosemary Wells, and the *Jumpstart Training Manual* from Pearson Custom Publishing. Pearson sponsors fundraisers, provides advertising in *The Financial Times*, and helps Jumpstart expand through outreach to potential university partners. Additionally, over one thousand Pearson employees are supporting Jumpstart and the Pearson Teacher Fellowship by volunteering in the preschools, collecting much needed resources and supplies for these communities, and mentoring Pearson Teacher Fellows. "Through these initiatives," says Kathleen Morgan, Manager of the Pearson-Jumpstart Partnership, "Pearson is encouraging college students to choose a career in teaching and helping

Jumpstart achieve its mission—to work toward the day every child in America enters school prepared to succeed" (Morgan, personal communication, June, 2004). Pearson/Allyn and Bacon Publishers will donate the profits from this book to Jumpstart.

On that note, we would like to celebrate all of the great people who work with young people. We thank Ed Greene, Montclair State University; Kathleen Morgan, Manager, Pearson–Jumpstart Partnership, and Kim Davenport, Jumpstart Vice President of Education and Training for their reviews of the manuscript. We thank the enthusiastic people involved in the Jumpstart program who offered their insights to us. We thank our friends, Darrell Morris, Linda Kucan, Dick Allington, and Alan Crawford for sharing their thoughts in these pages. We thank Mark Gearan for writing the foreword, and Aurora Martinez, our good friend and editor at Allyn and Bacon, who not only honchos good books to fruition, but obligingly keeps having children so we teachers can have kids to educate.

chapter one

Why Do We Need to Intervene?

When William Wordsworth wrote, "The child is father of the man," he meant that this early childhood classroom in front of us is the cradle of the future. Any one of these children will one day rock the world with an awesome song, choreograph a breathtaking ballet, negotiate peace in a troubled corner of the world, invent a treatment for leukemia, design an automobile everyone will love—be a caring teacher, an inspiring professor, a neighbor who helps kids with their homework.

But to move on from this classroom toward any of those happy futures, each child must develop a rich and supple grasp of the language we speak and hear and read and write. She must grow confident and clear in her thinking about the things that go on inside her and around her and beyond her. In order to think clearly about these things, she must know their names. And be able to read and write their names. And be able to take from and contribute to the flow of ideas that come to us through the spoken word and in written texts. In order to reach such a future, she will need language and literacy.

What Is the Problem?

American schools are some of the best in the world. Children in the primary grades in the United States rate among the world's very best readers, scoring second (only behind Finland) on one recent international comparison. Adult workers in the United States are the most productive anywhere, and the amount of earnings per capita in the United States is 25% above the world average. Workers in the United States are among the world's most creative and innovative. In an important measure of creative output, the United States leads every European country in the number of patents per capita (although we lag far behind Japan and Korea). Clearly our country and its educational system are doing many things right. But as we shall see, although the United States prides itself on being a land of opportunity for all, the chances for success in school—and for the successes in life that directly follow school—are not shared equally. If there is one key to success in school, it is literacy.

To the Reader We're about to tell you why we're worried about some young children who might not get off to a good start in their education, particularly as readers. Before you read our ideas, please pause for a minute and think ahead. What children are you worried about? That is, what factors do you think might make it harder for some children to learn to be readers?

This book has been written out of a concern that *although our average achievements remain high, far too many children in the United States are not learning language and literacy to an adequate degree.* To understand this concern, first note how the National Assessment of Educational Progress (NAEP) defines adequate reading:

> Fourth grade students performing at the *basic level* should demonstrate an understanding of the overall meaning of what they read . . . [T]hey should be able to make relatively obvious connections between the text and their own experiences, and extend the ideas in the text by making simple inferences. (NAEP, 1994, p. 42; emphasis added)

In the 2003 report of the NAEP, **two out of every five** fourth graders in the United States could not read at that basic level—and **two out of three** African American and Hispanic students tested could not read on the basic level (NAEP, 2003). The National Reading Panel summarizes the concern this way:

> 25 to 40% of American children are imperiled because they do not read well enough, quickly enough, or easily enough to ensure comprehension of their content subjects. (Snow, et al., 1998, p. 98)

Our successes, as individuals and as a country, often serve as blinders that prevent us from recognizing and internalizing the extent of the literacy problem in the United States.

So who are the children who are most likely to fail to read?

Risk Factors: Children Who Are Poor

It is hard for children to participate fully in school activities if they are poor. There are obvious reasons for this, such as insufficient nutrition, or the inability to pay for school supplies. Less obvious reasons are the myriad stress factors experienced by families and children who are poor. Many of these factors can affect concentration and learning. How many children are we talking about? In the United States, between 21% and 25% of children live in poverty (defined as 50% of the median income per person). That is three times as high as poverty rates for children in France and ten times the rate for children in Sweden (Luxembourg Income Study, 2000). In fact, when it comes to keeping children out of poverty, the United States ranks behind every industrialized country—and only slightly ahead of Mexico.

Risk Factors: Children from Minority Cultural Groups

Schools in America still have a long way to go when it comes to serving all of our children. There are huge differences in learning success among children in different states; among children in the inner cities, rural areas and the suburbs; and among children from different racial and economic groups (Grissmer, et al., 2000).

Unlike most countries in the world, education in the United States is managed by individual states, not nationally. If you were a teacher in Portugal, you would be paid essentially the same money whether you taught in the glitzy resort area of the Algarve, or in a rural village in the sparsely populated ranch country outside Castelho Branco. Your class sizes would be similar, as would be the resources available to you. That is not at all true in the United States, where teachers' salaries, class size, and classroom resources vary tremendously from state to state. And within each state, there can be huge differences in the amount of money available to schools in the suburbs, the inner city, and in rural areas, because school funding is based on real estate taxes.

Add to the economic disparities among schools two more factors. One factor concerns the socio-economic disparities between racial groups. Compared to white children, black and Hispanic children are three times as likely to be poor. Second, compared to white children, black and Hispanic children are two and three times as likely to come from single parent homes. Consider the data from the Urban Institute (1999), found in Table 1.1.

Risk Factors: Children in Racially Segregated Schools

Then add another factor: the racial segregation of American schools.

70.2% of the nation's black students now attend predominantly minority schools (minority enrollment of over 50%), up significantly from the low point of 62.9% in 1980. More than a third of the nation's black students (36.5%) attend schools with a minority enrollment of 90–100%. The proportion of black students in such schools has been rising consistently since 1986, when it was at a low point of 32.5%. . . .

Table 1.1   Stress Factors on Children's Lives, By Race

Population	White	Hispanic	Black
Children ages 0–17, as a percentage of the U.S. population	64.1	15.8	15.3
Children ages 0–17 living below the poverty level	9.9	31.5	35.4
Children ages 0–17 living in two-parent homes	72.1	59.9	28.6
Children ages 0–17 living in single-parent homes	17.0	29.4	54.7

Source: Sarah Staveteig and Alyssa Wigton (1999). *1999 Snapshots of America's Families II: Key Findings by Race and Ethnicity.* Urban Institute [http://www.urban.org/content/research/newfederalism/nsaf/snapshots/1999results/keyfindingsbyraceandethnicity/keyfindings.htm].

The most dramatic trends in segregation affect Latino students. While intense segregation for blacks is still 28 points below its 1969 level, it has actually grown 13.5 points for Latinos. In 1968, 23.1% of Latino students attended schools with a minority enrollment of 90–100%. In 1998, that number rose to 36.6% of Latino students. (Orfield & Yun, 1999)

An African American or Hispanic student in a white, middle-class school is likely to become a competent reader. But most African American children go to school with other African American children, in schools that are underfunded and under-resourced. The most proficient schools in America—and these mostly serve upper middle-class children—compare favorably with the best schools in the world. But there are also schools in some American cities in which children's reading scores are on a par with schools in Tanzania (Berliner, Biddle, and Bell, 1996).

If children's educational disadvantages persist into later years, it can be very, very difficult to make up the difference, as Senator Hillary Rodham Clinton (2004) points out:

The enormous needs of children who grow up in concentrated poverty and the dearth of highly qualified teachers in their schools mean that even dollar-equality per pupil, which is far from the reality in many communities, is not real equality in any meaningful sense. There are public schools that succeed in educating disadvantaged minority children—for example, the Maya Angelou Charter School in Washington, D.C., a city where half of all kids never finish high school. With small classes, a full-day program with breakfast, lunch, and dinner, and an army of volunteer tutors and mentors, almost all students at Maya Angelou earn a high school diploma, and 70 percent go on to college. Achieving these results costs about $25,000 per student—a figure that echoes a recent study of New York City public schools finding that "large central city districts must spend two to three times as much as the average district to reach the same performance standard."

My friends, you and I know that progress has a price. We are kidding ourselves, and our children, if we believe that real equality can be bought on the cheap. But the price is worth paying because investments in education are repaid in productivity, economic growth, and good citizenship; because the alternatives—unemployment, crime, and incarceration—are even more costly over a lifetime; and because the principle of equal opportunity in Brown v. Board of Education requires nothing less.

Even in mixed communities, if a child from a family that is not white and middle class goes to a school that serves children who are white and middle class, the lack of a cultural match will matter. Cultural mismatches are the stuff of humor in the hands of playwrights like George Bernard Shaw (*Pygmalion/My Fair Lady*) or actors like Eddie Murphy (*Beverly Hills Cop*). But cultural mismatches can be hard on kids.

Anthropologist Shirley Brice Heath spent ten years observing the ways families of different social classes use language and literacy in their households, and then examining what happens when their children arrive in school. The patterns Heath shows are amazing. For example, here is an observation of white working-class children whose parents go to the fundamentalist Christian church every Sunday. Only the preacher is allowed to read from the "Good Book" and only he is trusted to say what it means. On weeknights, the mothers dutifully read to their children before bedtime, but they shush the children firmly if they try to ask questions or try to comment on the book. The children are scolded if they create a tale from their imaginations. In these literal-minded households, there is little daylight between storytelling and lying.

The poor black children who live on the edge of town use language in a very different way from the poor white kids. The black children love to tell stories, recite chants, even make up poetry. Teegie, aged two and a half, makes up this story poem when he hears a church bell in the distance:

> *Way*
> *Far*
> *Now*
> *It a church bell*
> *Ringin'*
> *Dey singin'*
> > *Ringin'*
> *You hear it?*
> *I hear it*
> *Far*
> *Now*
> (Heath, 1983, p. 170)

The eight- and nine-year-old children around his neighborhood love to chant, and their chants are often salted by insults and taboo words:

> *Yo ma, yo ma*
> *Yo greasy greasy gran ma*
> *Got skinny legs 'n fat behin'*
> *Enuf to scare ol' Frankenstein.*
> (p. 175)

Or

> *Shit, God damn*
> *Git off yo' ass 'n jam.*
> (p. 177)

And when these children's parents read, it's often a collaborative event. For instance, one day, Lem's mother, Lillie Mae, reaches in the mailbox and pulls out a flyer from a local day care center. She reads the first paragraph aloud:

Lillie Mae: You hear this? It says Lem [her son, then two years old] might can get into Ridgeway, but I hafta have the papers ready and apply by next Friday.

Visiting friend: You ever been to Kent to get his birth certificate? [Friend is mother of three children already in school]

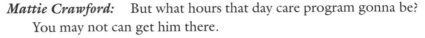

Mattie Crawford: But what hours that day care program gonna be? You may not can get him there.

Lillie Mae: They want the birth certificate? I got his vaccination papers.

Annie Mae: Sometimes they take that, 'cause they can 'bout tell the age from those early shots.

Visiting friend: But you better get it, 'cause you gotta have it when he go to school anyway.

Lillie Mae: But it says here they don't know what hours yet. How am I gonna get over to Kent? How much does it cost? Lemme see if the program costs anything. (She reads aloud part of the letter.) (Heath, 1983, p. 197)

Home background in language and literacy made a difference before the children entered school. Both working-class white and working-class black children were described by their teachers as difficult to teach. Teachers used these terms to describe children from one of the groups:

"Disrespectful."

". . . If they don't get it from me, they'll flit about the room until them find someone who'll tell 'em."

"Verbally and physically aggressive."

And these terms to describe children from the other group:

"Shows little imagination."

"Respond to low level questions minimally, with little imagination or extension of ideas."

"Neither girls nor boys want to step out and take initiative on anything."

(From Heath, 1983, pp. 268–269).

You can easily tell which children were being talked about in each case, can't you?

Educators have focused on ways to reach children from poor African American families. For instance, Lisa Delpit (1995), a former teacher and a literacy expert, observed that African American children were at a disadvantage in the kinds of child-centered "workshop environments" that emerged in U.S. literacy classes in the 1980s. In the same class where white children had their creativity stimulated through this particular teaching approach, African American children seemed to be waiting in vain for explicit directions. African American children certainly could succeed in learning to read and write, said Delpit, but cultural differences meant that those children thrive on direct and explicit instructions. The more open environment of workshop-based teaching just leaves them directionless. Delpit argued that to withhold explicit instruction from black children amounts to a conspiracy against them. In the strong words of a black colleague of Delpit's from Philadelphia, "This is just another one of those racist ploys to keep our kids out" (Delpit, 1995, p. 16).

No one has stepped forward to speak up for working-class white children. Often, the parents of the working-class white children experience the cultural and linguistic gulf between home and school as a moral divide, and they take their children out of the public schools and teach them at home (Bauman, 2001).

Risk Factors: Children Who Speak Languages Other Than English

Another group of children who often have difficulty learning to read are those whose home language is not English. The number of these "English Language Learners" has increased more than 70% in the last decade, so that today, nearly one child in ten in U.S. classrooms is an English Language Learner. For the total school population, that's 4.5 million children. These are mostly young children, in the primary grades. No longer are they concentrated mainly in California, Texas, South Florida, and New York City. Now, English Language Learners are in classrooms all across the United States, with Nevada, Iowa, and North Carolina experiencing large influxes of these students recently. Eighty percent of language learners are Spanish speakers, but in some schools, speakers of many other languages are found— even in the same classrooms.

English Language Learners vary considerably in their exposure to both English and literacy. Some young children have fluency in the first language and are well on their way to learning to read it. Other children learn English as a second language, and learn to read in English without difficulty. (The son of one of the authors, Iuliu, came to the United States from Romania at the age of four without knowing English. While he continued to speak Romanian at home with his mother and sister, at school he spoke only English, and within a year he could speak English fluently. By the end of first grade, his reading took off, and now in second grade he is a voracious reader: at the age of seven he has finished four of the *Harry Potter* books, and is half way through the fifth.)

Often, however, being an English Language Learner combines with socio-economic factors, so that these children may also be poor and their parents may be under-educated.

Either way, children without adequate knowledge of the English language may experience difficulty learning to read in English. On the most basic level, reading means deciphering groups of letters to read words, and understanding the words. Reading cannot work successfully if children do not have experiences using and understanding those words. The National Reading Panel (Snow, et al., 1998) identified limited English ability as a strong predictor of difficulty in learning to read in young children.

These four factors—financial disparity between schools, socio-economic disparity between races, racial segregation of the schools, and the struggle to learn the language of the school—add up to inequality of educational opportunity.

Now, let's look more carefully at a couple of factors in young children's lives that may make learning to read difficult.

Alan Crawford
Emeritus Professor UCLA

Working with ESL Students

English language learners have many strengths—proficiency in their mother tongue, in their culture, and the background knowledge that underlies it. But tutors who work to strengthen the learning abilities of these children usually must work with them in English, especially if several languages and cultures are represented in the group. There are many valuable activities that these children can engage in to strengthen their English language skills and become more ready for reading later, but two key activities are readalouds and conversation with comprehensible input.

Risk Factors: Children with Language Limitations and Reading Difficulties

We have said that children whose home language is other than English may have reading difficulties, but native English speakers experience language-related problems learning to read as well. For one thing, English-speaking children from poorer and less educated families get far fewer opportunities for *verbal interaction* than do children from middle-class families (Hart and Risley, 1995). Verbal interaction means having someone talk to you, carefully tailoring the nature and content of her or his speech to your growing capacity.

As background to this idea, consider that all during the 1970s and 1980s there was an outpouring of discoveries of the amazing synchronicity of mothers' talk with children's growing abilities (e.g., Stern 1977; Shaffer, 1977). These studies gave the impression that parents' interacting verbally with their children was natural and universal. But when later researchers observed families in the under-represented parts of the community, examples of rich and well-adapted adult-to-child speech were not so easy to find.

Shirley Brice Heath's work (1983), already cited above, found that working-class black mothers did almost none of the face-to-face play that had been documented in white middle-class families. One of the mothers explained that she thought it was better to let the child figure things out for himself:

> *White folks uh hear dey kids say sump'n, dey say it back to 'em, dey aks 'em 'gain 'n 'gain 'bout things, like they 'posed to be born knowin'. You think I can tell Teegie [her one year old son] all he gotta know to get along? He just gotta be keen, keep his eyes open, don't he be sorry."* (Heath, 1983, p. 84)

Hart and Risley (1995) found differences in children's chances to talk in different social groups. Huge differences. Their research team took one-hour monthly snapshots of the language used around children in professional families, working-class families, and families on welfare. Their findings are displayed in Table 1.2.

Children from families on welfare were talked to only a third as much as children from professional families, and children from working-class families were talked to only half as much. Children's language developed or failed to develop in proportion to the language that adults used with them. The children used no grammatical structures and few words that the parents didn't use when talking with them. Other studies have shown the results of limited

Table 1.2   Differences in Language Exposure of Preschool Children

	Professional Families	Working-Class Families	Families on Welfare
Words spoken to the children per hour	3000	1,400	750
Total words addressed to a child in the first four years	50 million	30 million	15 million
Verbal encouragements from parents ("Yes, that's good!")	750,000	300,000	100,00
Verbal prohibitions from parents ("Stop!" "Don't!" "Quit!")	130,000	170,000	280,000

Source: Adapted from Hart and Risley (1995).

language input in the early years: by first grade, children from low-income under-educated families have *half* the vocabulary of children from middle-class families. Poor children continue to fall behind middle-class children, so that verbal middle-class third graders have more sophisticated vocabularies than less verbal twelfth graders (Beck, McKeown, and Kucan, 2002).

Why does vocabulary matter? Because words have a Janus-like quality of representing what children have already learned and what they are about to learn. Looking backwards, vocabulary represents the accumulation of concepts and categories into which children's thinking has been differentiated—that is, it is an index of their accumulation of knowledge. Looking forward, because we tend to notice what we can name (Brown, 1954), vocabulary represents the wealth of phenomena that children will be able to perceive, categorize, communicate, and remember. That is, vocabulary represents much of children's potential for learning.

Vocabulary pays off early in school by making it easier for a child to learn to read (Snow, et al., 1998). Knowing many words helps reading in three ways. First, the whole point of puzzling through letters and sounds is to make meaning from what is read, and children who do not know most of the words won't make much sense of the text. Second, a limited vocabulary is associated with limited world knowledge. Understanding what they read means that children must already know at least some orienting ideas of what they are reading about. Because each word in a person's vocabulary functions as a marker for concepts—and makes it more likely that children will notice and be able to think about the thing named (Brown, 1955)—a limited vocabulary may hamper knowledge acquisition. Third, limited vocabulary also hampers rapid access to prior knowledge—that is, it is harder to articulate and use what you know if you don't have names for it. It's not surprising that tests of verbal intelligence (I.Q.) focus heavily on children's vocabulary.

Limited expressive language is another aspect of development that hinders children's success in learning to read. Limited expressive or spoken language is most often measured in the average length of children's sentences. That is because with length comes complexity, and with complexity comes important shades of meaning. Note the difference between "I hurt him" and "I will hurt him"; or "Start singing" and "Start singing when I give the signal." Both pairs have different meanings; but it requires more advanced language development to say or understand the second one. Without this language development, there is confusion.

So far in our list of important language-related accomplishments we have identified vocabulary and the knowledge of the world that vocabulary encodes, along with grammar and the shades of meaning and logical relationships that grammar encodes. But there is another important aspect of children's language experience that makes a difference in children's success in learning. In the Hart and Risley (1995) study, the researchers recorded how often the children from the different families were praised and encouraged, as opposed to criticized and discouraged. Children from professional families received nearly **eight times** as much praise and encouragement as did the children from welfare families, and three times as much praise and encouragement as children from working-class families. Here is what they thought their findings meant:

> The differences we saw between families seemed to reflect the cultural priorities parents casually transmit through talking. In the professional families the extraordinary amount of talk, the many different words, and the greater richness of nouns, modifiers, and past-tense verbs in parent utterances suggested a culture concerned with names, relationships, and recall. Parents seemed to be preparing their children to participate in a culture concerned with symbols and analytic problem solving. . . . In the welfare families, the lesser amount of talk with its more frequent parent-initiated topics, imperatives, and prohibitions suggested a culture concerned with established customs. To teach socially acceptable behavior, language rich in nouns and modifiers was not called for; obedience, politeness, and conformity were more likely to be keys to survival. (Hart and Risley, 1995, pp. 133–134)

But we don't want conformity and obedience from poor children. We want them to break out of the marginalized economic and political roles their parents have been allowed to play in our country. We want them to be able to grow up to be whatever they want to be: poets, inventors, organizers, healers, movers and shakers.

To the Reader So what should you take away from all this? You can't overestimate the importance of language in a child's life—not just for reading but for learning in general, and even for expanding a child's sense of possibilities. As a tutor, you will make a big difference in the life of a child by talking with her—showing her things that interest her, engaging her in activities that are stimulating, and interweaving natural talk throughout the whole experience. We will have more to say about this later on.

Risk Factors: Children from Under-Supportive Home Literacy Environments

Children's home environments matter in how well they support children as they learn to read and write. The National Reading Panel (Snow, et al., 1998) points to four important ways that homes encourage children to learn to read.

One way is by placing value on literacy. Children want to be good at the things that please their parents, the things that parents are good at. If parents take obvious pleasure in reading—if they spend part of every day reading, and often stop and share passages aloud with each other, children will want to read.

Another way families encourage children to learn to read is by encouraging them to achieve at reading. Parents who press their children to achieve set expectations that are just challenging enough, give them support to meet those challenges, and then praise them when they succeed. For example, when reading aloud with a child, a parent says "Now I read those first couple of pages. *You* read this page—you can do it. . . . Good!" From these interactions, children not only learn about literacy, they learn how to meet challenges, and to work hard for success. They become motivated to be better readers and come to enjoy reading as a recreational activity.

A third way families help children to read is by having literacy materials available. Children not only need to have books read to them; they need to page through them on their own and explore them—get to know them. Parents of young children who learn to read easily in school have children's books in the home that they have either bought or borrowed from the library. They may subscribe to children's magazines, and buy posters related to particular stories that appeal to their children.

The fourth and most important way for parents to help children learn to read, of course, is to read to them. When parents read to children, teach them songs, and provide them with recorded books to page along with, children

- Learn what books are like
- Learn concepts about print
- Learn vocabulary
- Develop personal interests
- Increase their comprehension of language—especially the special "de-contextualized" language of books
- Increase their attention span
- Learn to enjoy books

Dick Allington
President-elect—International Reading Association

Importance of Families and Home Environment

I've spent most of my career worrying about children who were being left behind in reading. These children were often from lower-income families and they began school "behind." They began behind in the sense that they had had far fewer literacy experiences than other more advantaged children. Fewer opportunities to be read aloud to. Fewer opportunities to play with magnetic letters and pencils and paper. Fewer opportunities to learn nursery rhymes. Too many schools seemed unready for these children and responded by labeling the children. Too few schools responded by providing a richer and more personalized educational environment.

It's not surprising that better educated, middle-class parents read to their children far more on the average than do poorer and under-educated parents. But the good news, though, is that parents in all income and educational groups are reading to their children more than they were ten years ago (see Table 1.2). Parents are clearly getting the message that reading to their children is a good and helpful thing.

But we should keep in mind that just reading to children is not enough. It matters *how* adults read to children. Children have greater enjoyment, and learn more from the book-reading experience, when adults read with children interactively (Heath, 1983; Whitehurst and Lonigan, 1998). That means reading with an animated voice. Creating suspense. Pointing to things and asking for comments. Asking the child questions, and encouraging her to wonder, predict, approve or condemn—and above all, to talk. We will have much more to say about these things in later chapters.

Not all children get enough of these four kinds of encouragement. If a family is poor, if the parents have less education, or if there is only one parent in the home, children may have fewer of these family supports going for them (NCES, 2003). These *home literacy factors* are huge benefits and they add up to success in school. The National Center for Educational Statistics found that the more home literacy factors three- to five-year-old children had going for them, the higher their reading scores at the end of kindergarten (see Table 1.3).

Brigit Beyea
Executive Director of Jumpstart NY/Mid-Atlantic Region

Language Development

Children who miss out on key language and literacy skills in the early years face extraordinary challenges later in their education. Young children need adults to help them use emergent writing skills—those scribbles across a page—to be inspired to turn those into what become letters. They need adults to read to them in ways that get the children to tell the stories, what's on the page or what's in their hearts, so they'll develop a joy of reading and learning.

Table 1.3   Mean Home Literacy Index and Mean Fall Kindergarten Reading Scale Score of Young Children Enrolled in Kindergarten for the First Time, by Selected Characteristics: 1998–99

Selected Characteristics	Mean Home Literacy Index	Mean Fall Kindergarten Reading Scale Score
Total	**2.9**	**22.2**
Sex		
Male	2.8	21.6
Female	3.1	22.8
Race/ethnicity[1]		
Asian	2.7	26.7
Black	2.4	20.1
White	3.2	23.3
Other[2]	2.7	20.1
Hispanic	2.5	19.5
Mother's home language		
English	3.0	22.3
Other than English	2.2	20.0
Mother's education		
Less than high school	2.1	17.3
High school diploma or equivalent	2.6	20.3
Some college, including vocational/technical	3.1	22.5
Bachelor's degree	3.5	26.2
Graduate/first-professional degree	3.7	28.3
Family type		
Two-parent household	3.1	23.0
None or one-parent household	2.6	19.8
Poverty status[3]		
Below poverty threshold (poor)	2.3	18.1
At or above poverty threshold (nonpoor)	3.1	23.1
Between 100 and 200 percent of the poverty threshold	2.7	20.2
Above 200 percent of the poverty threshold	3.2	24.3

[1]Black includes African American, and Hispanic includes Latino. Race categories exclude Hispanic origin unless specified.
[2]Other includes Pacific Islander or Native Hawaiin, American Indian or Alaskan Native, and more than one race.
[3]See supplement note 3 for additional information on poverty status.

Source: U.S. Department of Education, NCES, Early Childhood Longitudinal Study, Kindergarten Class of 1998–99 (ECLS-K), Base Year Public-Use Data File, 1998–99, February 2001.

Risk Factors: Children Whose Parents Are Less Involved in Their Education

There are many ways parents can be involved in their children's education. They can do the kinds of family literacy activities we have already mentioned: reading to their children, talking to them interactively, listening to their stories, and singing songs with them. They can bring children's books into the home. They can regulate their children's television watching and make efforts to talk to their children about what they watch. They can take their children to museums, or simply point out things to them as they walk around town.

When children reach school age, parents can set aside quiet space and time for the children to do their school work. They can make sure children complete the assignments that come home from school. They can offer help on homework when children need it.

They can communicate with the child's teacher by attending parent conferences, and give the teacher insights about their child's interests and personal characteristics that may prove useful to the teacher in constructing lessons for the child. When necessary, they can support the teacher in reinforcing a behavior regime for the child.

When parents cooperate with the schools, children's achievement goes up, attendance goes up, and drop-out rates go down. But parents differ markedly in the extent to which they cooperate with the schools. The National Center for Educational Statistics (2003) recently reported:

> While 72 percent of schools with a low concentration of poverty reported that "most or all" parents attended the school open house, 28 percent of schools with a high poverty concentration reported such high parent attendance. Similar differences were found on this variable when schools with low minority enrollments were compared to those with high minority enrollments (63 versus 30 percent).

Schools with 50% poverty enrollments report these reasons for lack of parent involvement:

- Lack of parent education to help with schoolwork
- Cultural differences
- Socioeconomic differences

- Language differences between parents and staff
- Parent attitudes about the school
- Staff attitudes toward parents
- Concerns about safety in the area after school hours (NCES 2003)

Many children have parents who are poorly educated themselves. Parents who do not read well are not able to support their children's learning, because they cannot easily read to them or help them with homework. They may participate infrequently in school activities—at least in part because they may not be able to understand the written materials that are sent home from school,[1] but also out of feelings of inadequacy. For instance, one parent told one of the authors that even though she loved volunteering as an aide in her son's Head Start classroom, she would feel shut out when he moved into kindergarten the following year—even though the kindergarten class was in the same building. She said she wouldn't feel welcome. And besides, she asked with obvious worry, what would happen if they asked her to read something aloud to the children?

Some parents feel not just embarrassed but alienated from the school because they had negative experiences there. Says one father:

> *They expect me to go to school so they can tell me my kid is stupid or crazy. They've been telling me that for three years, so why should I go and hear it again? They don't do anything. They just tell me my kid is bad. See, I've been there. I know. And it scares me. They called me a boy in trouble but I was a troubled boy. Nobody helped me because they liked it when I didn't show up. If I was gone for the semester, fine with them. I dropped out nine times. They wanted me gone.* (Finders & Lewis, 1994, p. 51)

Happily, when parents are encouraged to get involved in their children's education while they are young, they are more likely to keep up the habit later. (Head Start Evaluation). Boosting parent involvement is a crucial goal of early intervention projects for young children.

---

[1]We sometimes have classes run readability tests on notes addressed to parents that come home from elementary schools. They usually test out at an eighth- to twelfth-grade reading level, well beyond the reach of many parents of children in those schools.

To the Reader Over the last several pages we have talked about what homes and families contribute to language learning and literacy. You may be saying, "But what does that have to do with me? I'm a college volunteer!" Well, for one thing, we hope it shows you how precious your time with your child will be, and we hope it suggests things you can do (Talk! Interact! Read! Draw! Talk! Explore! Talk!). For another thing, it underscores the importance of including parents in their child's education in some way. Tutors in the Jumpstart program, for instance, send letters home to the children's parents, telling them what they have been doing together. Many tutors report that parents respond with real interest and enthusiasm—and often get interested in doing some of these things themselves.

Why Are We Concentrating Our Attention on Young Children?

In recent years, educators have focused special attention on younger children for the simple reason that early experiences matter. Children who enter reading instruction well prepared are more likely to respond well to that instruction. And children who are successful in learning to read in first grade tend to keep making progress in literacy from then on. The reverse is also true. Children who enter school with limitations in language development and early literacy concepts tend not to respond well to reading instruction. And their poor start may grow into reading failure.

When Connie Juel (1994) followed 56 children from first grade through fourth grade, she found that most of the children who were well prepared as they entered the first grade continued to make progress in learning to read throughout the study. But nearly all of the children who entered first grade behind their classmates had failed to close the gap three years later. In fact, their deficits, which were comparatively minor in first grade, had become patterns of failure: inadequate knowledge of component skills, ineffective reading strategies, and discouraged attitudes.

Keith Stanovich (1986) has called these patterns "Matthew Effects," after the Biblical observation that the rich shall get richer and the poor shall get poorer. When this principle is applied to learning to read, it means that

Dana Nielson
Preschool Teacher—Geneva Lakefront Child Center

Desire for Independence

I have been a preschool teacher for 17 years and have been working with children since I was twelve years old. Overall, I have worked with children for the majority of my life. One thing I notice about working with this particular age group is how their thinking begins to develop. Their attitude shows a lot about their desire to be independent. From "No, I don't need help" to "I can do it on my own," I see a lot of these children wanting to do things on their own without the help of adults.

the concepts about language and literacy children bring with them into kindergarten and first grade make it easy and natural for them to learn each new ability they need, so they willingly practice reading because they feel good at it and they enjoy it. But the reverse also happens. If a child's early literacy concepts are in short supply, she will struggle to acquire each new ability that literacy demands. Difficulty will soon breed aversion, and the child will not practice in order to improve his or her abilities. (In a future chapter, we will make it clear exactly what abilities we are talking about that build upon each other as children learn to read.)

Overall, this is a pretty sobering picture. Children have a far greater chance of learning the basics of literacy in the early grades if they already have an accumulation of experience with language and print by the time they come to school. If they fail to get off to a good start in the very first years of school, they are unlikely to close the gap. They are unlikely to become proficient readers. What then?

What Difference Does Literacy Make?

What happens if she doesn't learn language and literacy, in adequate measure? Advertising campaigns show us images of the embarrassed grown-up, standing on a city street with a decoy newspaper under his arm that he can't read, staring at a street sign he can't decipher, afraid someone will recognize him for an illiterate. Such people exist, but the problem of limited literacy is

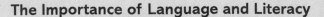

Debbie Peduzzi
Site Manager for Jumpstart Pittsburgh

The Importance of Language and Literacy

Language and literacy are fundamental topics for preschool children to learn before they head off to kindergarten and the rest of their education. Too many statistics have shown that children have gone through years of school without being at their "typical" reading level. Language and literacy development is a timely skill to learn. It is not developed overnight. I think it is important for children to learn through interactions that they have with other children and adults. Children should feel comfortable about their environment. If they feel this comfort, then they will be more prepared to move on to learning other skills such as phonemic and phonological awareness.

far more widespread and more subtle than the isolated person who is afraid others will find out he doesn't know what he should. One in every three or four adults in America—sixty million people[2]—read and write so poorly that they seriously limit their opportunities. Exacerbating these problems is that fact that the literacy demands of society continue to rise.

Large-scale studies in the United States have shown that as a whole, adults' earning levels rise and fall in lock-step with their reading levels.[3] The better you read and write, the more money you make, and the more likely you are to be employed, to hold a professional job, to have good health, to stay off public assistance, and to stay out of jail. It goes the other way, too. Those who are in menial jobs, unemployed, on public assistance, or in the penal system are disproportionately people with low reading and writing skills.

In two senses, individuals with limited literacy speak a different language from those with greater literacy. This is often literally true because those with limited English skills are among those with the lowest literacy skills. But it is true in a more subtle way. People who do not read much miss out on a large body of words that come to us almost exclusively through print. Words like "isolated," "probability," "prohibit," and "null and void"

[2]Kozol, *Illiterate America.*
[3]National Center for Educational Statistics. *The National Adult Literacy Survey.* (1992).

are found in print, but are almost never used in oral language. They are not used in conversations or heard on television. Yet each of these words casts light on a slice of experience that we could not easily grasp without having the word. Not knowing what an "isolated case" is can lead a person into superstition. Not understanding "probability" keeps people spending their grocery money on the lottery. Not understanding the word "prohibit" can land people in jail; and not knowing what "null and void" means can leave a family without a lease on an apartment, without a place to live.[4]

But unlike the image of the furtive adult illiterate worried that his secret will get out, the people with the lowest levels of literacy on national surveys say they don't see literacy as a problem. They rarely report asking others to help them read or write something, and—unlike statisticians—they don't link low literacy with a limited range of choices in their lives.[5] That means that teachers have to face a double task: helping children learn to read, and helping children and their families *value* reading.

> **To the Reader** Whew! Thanks for bearing with us through all that. It can get a little gloomy focusing on what can hold some children back, but we must understand these things so we will see how important this work is, and so we will know how to best direct our energies.
>
> Now, imagine you are a site leader on a tutoring project and you are explaining to a new group of tutors why they should take the job seriously. From what you have read so far, see if you can construct a good argument.

And Now for Some Good News

The rest of this book is about the good news. And there really are grounds for encouragement.

First, if we know so much about what is missing from the lives of children who get off to a poor start in literacy, then we ought to know how to help. And we do. Descriptive studies of what children need to know in order to learn to read have swept away a huge amount of nonsense and showed us what we need to know.

[4]David Olsen, quoted in Stanovich, 1992.
[5]National Adult Literacy Survey, *op. cit.*

Second, teaching strategies have been designed that really do help develop children's language. While we have long realized that children need preschool education, now we know that even four-year-olds need a strong literacy component to their education. In the past dozen years, venerable programs like Head Start have added strong emergent literacy components. And they work.

Third, tutoring programs have been developed to add heft to preschool programs' language and literacy development curricula. Jumpstart (2003) is one such program. Studies have shown that children who received the one-on-one tutoring from Jumpstart volunteers learned language and literacy concepts at a faster rate than their classmates who lacked such help. These results are especially impressive when you recognize that the children who were identified for help under the Jumpstart program were chosen because they were developing more slowly than their peers.

On the federal level, America Reads has mobilized thousands of college students to tutor one-on-one in the public schools. And one state-wide effort—the Ohio Literacy Initiative—has fielded over 20,000 volunteer tutors to help children learn to read.

If you are reading this book, chances are that you are one of those volunteers, or are contemplating becoming one. Let's get on with it, then. Somewhere a child is waiting for you!

Rob Waldron
President and CEO of Jumpstart

Jumpstart Summary

Jumpstart supplements the development of children who are identified as falling behind their peers, and seeks to enhance their language and literacy, their social skills, and their initiative-taking. Our activities tap into children's interests and the power of play: creative play fosters brain development, helps children become innovative thinkers, and helps build the skills necessary for success in school and throughout life.

chapter two

What Are Some Ways Children Develop?

How will these children grow up? Is there a series of stages they will go through, or will the process be different for each of them? Will some experiences help them more than others? Will they rely upon adults to teach them how to do, how to be—or can they be left largely alone to "just grow"?

Human development is a hard thing to conceptualize, so it shouldn't be surprising that people use metaphors to describe it. Shakespeare compared the stages of human life to the acts of a play:

All the world's a stage,
And all the men and women merely players:
They have their exits and their entrances;
And one man in his time plays many parts,
His acts being seven ages. At first the infant,
Mewling and puking in the nurse's arms.
And then the whining school-boy, with his satchel
And shining morning face, creeping like snail
Unwillingly to school. And then the lover,
Sighing like furnace, with a woeful ballad
Made to his mistress' eyebrow. Then a soldier,
Full of strange oaths and bearded like the pard,
Jealous in honour, sudden and quick in quarrel,
Seeking the bubble reputation
Even in the cannon's mouth. And then the justice,
In fair round belly with good capon lined,
With eyes severe and beard of formal cut,
Full of wise saws and modern instances;
And so he plays his part. The sixth age shifts
Into the lean and slipper'd pantaloon,
With spectacles on nose and pouch on side,
His youthful hose, well saved, a world too wide
For his shrunk shank; and his big manly voice,
Turning again toward childish treble, pipes
And whistles in his sound. Last scene of all,
That ends this strange eventful history,
Is second childishness and mere oblivion,
Sans teeth, sans eyes, sans taste, sans everything.
(As You Like It—Act II Scene 7)

To the Reader We once knew a first grade teacher who began the year by asking the children to reach across their heads with their right hands and touch their left ears. Those who could do this were placed in reading groups, and she began teaching them to read. The others were given pails and sent to the sand box for a few more weeks.

Now there was a theory behind this. The teacher believed that there was a direct relationship between the growth of children's bodies and the growth of their minds: if their arms were long enough, their brains must have matured, too—and they were ready to learn to read. (Bear in mind that babies are born with relatively large heads, and the rest of the body grows faster through childhood in proportion to the head.)

Surely, you also have some implicit theory about how children learn to think and learn to talk. That theory is likely to guide what you do when you interact with children. This chapter and the next one are meant to give you some research-based materials to inform your personal theory.

John Locke, an English philosopher who inspired the American *Declaration of Independence*, imagined every child's mind to be like a blank chalkboard, a *tabula rasa*, on which teachers and other adults could write whatever they wished (1689/1994). In the psychological version of the empty chalkboard, the Russian Ivan Pavlov thought of children as dogs who could be taught to salivate when they heard a bell; and the Americans John Watson (1926/1998) and B.F. Skinner (1971/2002) compared children to pigeons who could be trained to play ping pong or steer guided missiles if given the right kind of stimulus and reward.

Others gave children more credit for their own destiny. Erik Erikson (1993)—a Danish-born portrait painter, Montessori teacher, and self-taught psychologist—thought children were like acorns: the blueprint of their development was present at birth in each one. But Erikson also recognized that experience played a part. Like an acorn that lands on fertile ground or barren; the sapling that is nourished by rains or parched; and the mature oak that stands alone in a peaceful yard or crowded in a forest, bent by strong winds, carved upon by lovers, and scorched by brush fires, Erikson thought children's development is shaped as much by our experiences in

Erik Erikson's Eight Ages of Man

Birth–age 2	Basic trust vs. basic mistrust	If children develop secure attachments to one or more caregivers, they will have the basis of confidence that will help them explore their environment, learn about the world, and form other relationships.
Peaks between ages 2 and 4	Autonomy vs. Shame and doubt	If children have found security, when the teeth erupt and toilet training begins, they may confidently form concepts of themselves as separate beings from their caregivers.
Peaks between ages 4 and 6	Initiative vs. guilt	If children have found security, and their need for autonomy within relationships has been successfully negotiated, they may feel their oats, spread their wings, and thrust themselves into experiences without feeling that they are doing something wrong.
Peaks between ages 6 and 13	Industry vs. inferiority	If school-age children feel secure, autonomous, and capable of initiative, when the time comes to become good at tasks that adults value, they will apply themselves fully and successfully.
Peaks between ages 13 and 21	Identity vs. role confusion	If the adolescents have achieved a sense of security, autonomy, initiative, and industry, then they will know themselves—by who their people are, and by what they do.
Peaks between ages 22 and 28	Intimacy vs. isolation	If young adults have achieved all the foregoing, they will be able to enter deep and intimate relationships with others.
Peaks between ages 45 and 50	Generativity vs. stagnation	If the previous stages have been negotiated successfully, middle aged adults will cheerfully shoulder the responsibility to look out for both the younger and older generations.
Age 60–	Integrity vs. despair	If the previous stages have been traversed successfully, in old age these people will have achieved wisdom, a view of "the big picture," and a sense of oneness with others who have shared the human experience.

Source: Eric Erikson, *Childhood and Society.* New York: Norton, 1993.

society as by our genetic blueprint. Children's maturation, Erikson wrote, proceeds from stage to stage propelled by their growth, but at each stage what happens to the child from his or her social experience makes an influential difference in the child's later growth (see the box on page 28).

Piaget, Vygotsky, and Constructivism

A Swiss psychologist with training in biology, Jean Piaget (Singer, 1996) went further in giving the child credit for inventing herself. He thought of a child as an adaptive system—an organism bent on functioning in its own environment. The child-as-organism acquires and refines ideas about the world upon each encounter with a new thing; and with each change in its concepts, it gains a more elaborated potential for making sense of all encounters from that moment on.

To be more precise, Piaget theorized that when a child acts on an object—and the key word here is *act*, because children must be active in order to learn—she may form a *scheme* for it. A scheme is like a mental image or template, or concept. The word "image" doesn't quite fit, though, because some of our schemes are physical acts—like your scheme for turning the knob on your bedroom door, or slipping the key in the ignition and starting your car. Children use their schemes to navigate the world. They use them to recognize their mothers, yucky things, dogs, objects that burn to the touch, and cars. And the more they use their schemes to interpret things, the more they refine their schemes and differentiate them; for example, they learn a goat is a goat and not a dog, and so on.

But all that seemed a little too random for the Russian psychologist, Lev Vygotsky (1978). Vygotsky thought culture—and grown-ups—had to play a role in this concept formation. He agreed with Piaget that children took their experiences and formed them into concepts that they use in making sense of future experiences. But he saw a danger that children's random or "spontaneous concepts" could be off the wall. He was right.

Jill and Peter DeVilliers (1975) gave a fine example of a spontaneous concept in the language of their one-year-old. The boy called the family dog, Nancy, by his original name for her, "Nunu"; but he also said "Nunu" when he rubbed his hand on the shag carpet in the living room (probably because it was soft and furry like Nancy), when he had his hair brushed (because the brush scratched him like Nancy's claws), and even when he saw a ripe olive atop a neighboring diner's salad in a fancy restaurant (because the olive was wet, black, shiny, and round like Nancy's nose!). This boy was apparently associating a group of otherwise unrelated impressions with the name "Nunu." And that, Vygotsky warns us, is what much of children's conceptualizing is like.

Vygotsky realized that a child needs a competent language speaker present at the moment he is forming new concepts. That person should supply the proper name for the thing the child is discovering, so the child can form a *scientific concept* and not a spontaneous one. Unlike the spontaneous concept "Nunu" (see above), the scientific concept *dog* would name a class of four-legged furry animals that bark, that include the family dog, Nunu. If adults interact with children as they explore the world, and if they use the language of the educated community at just those moments each child is noticing something, then those children will gain not only the vocabulary of the educated community, but also the system of categories of knowledge that is valued in that community.

If you look closely at Vygotsky's description of learning, you will see that the initiative still comes from the child, with close participation of the adult. It is the child who is exploring and discovering; the adult follows the child's lead, and phases language in with the child's own thinking. For successful learning to happen, the child cannot merely discover, and the adult cannot simply teach. The child must be exploring, and the adult must track along with those actions and play her part with just the right words.

The title of Vygotsky's most famous book is *Thought and Language,* because to Vygotsky, the two develop together. Vocabulary is learned at the moment categories of reality are perceived. The acquisition of language channels and organizes thinking, and nails down perceptions so they can be noticed again, recalled, and communicated.

Under the influence of Vygotsky, researchers have come to notice the interconnection between children's acts of discovery and adults' carefully structured assistance. This assistance has come to be called *scaffolding*—it's the temporary help adults provide that is calibrated to complement and not supplant the children's own initiatives at discovery. The help adults provide is said to work within children's *zone of proximal development*. It is most instructive when it co-occurs with the children's acts of discovery, when it occurs at a moment of readiness to learn, or as an answer to an unspoken question.

It's no wonder that those who have watched carefully as young children learn language and concepts have used another metaphor: *the dance.*

How Do Children Learn to Talk?

The miracle of language learning seems to parallel some of the accounts of children's development we have already seen. Those who call attention to genetic predispositions to learn will find much to support their thinking in children's language learning. Learning language relies on some things that *are* innate. Babies appear to come into the world "pre-wired" with a set of capacities that makes it almost certain that they will learn language. For example, newborn babies just a few days old:

- will turn their heads and look toward the source of a sound;
- prefer patterned and varied sounds, like human voices, to random noises like buzzes and clicks;
- synchronize the movements of their bodies so that they "track along with" the rhythms of the speech they hear;
- can perceive extremely subtle distinctions in speech, such as the difference between the beginning consonant sounds in "bat" and "pat"—a difference that boils down to a 40/1000ths of a second delay in the vibration of the vocal chords;
- prefer high-pitched voices to low-pitched voices (but their fathers and even their ten-year old big brothers adopt high-pitched voices when they talk to babies!).

All of these "adjustments" in the babies' senses make it almost inevitable that they will be able to enter the dance of language with a human caregiver, maybe even a female one!

Linguist Noam Chomsky (1975) has argued that in addition to being pre-tuned to the right stimuli, babies are also "pre-wired" with the ability to examine the language they hear around them, tease out its patterns, and use those patterns to shape their own utterances. For example, two-year-olds are famous for saying "I got two *foots.*" And Iuliu, at age six, said "Don't worry, Mom. I'm hold-onning," after his mother told him to "hold on" during a windy sailboat ride. You can see that the two-year-old is aware that we say "more than one" by adding a /s/ (or /z/ or /Iz/) to a noun. And you can see that Iuliu knows that verbs add *–ing* to show that action is going on in the present. Both have figured out rules of grammar from listening to adult speech and teasing out the patterns. You can't say they are merely imitating what they hear adults say, because children often say sentences that adults *wouldn't* say.

But children who are learning language need the help of adults, too. We have horrifying accounts of children raised in social isolation who barely learn to talk (Aitchison, 1998). We also have detailed accounts of children learning to talk in different kinds of families, and what the parents contributed clearly made a difference. What do children need from adults in order to learn language?

"Motherese": How Adults Support Children's Language Learning

When adults are helping infants learn to talk, it is remarkable how much of this "help" comes naturally and unconsciously. Take the case of a mother engaged in face-to-face play with a six-month-old child.

- The mother gazes into the child's face and raises the pitch of her voice to a high register.
- She makes swooping changes from low to high, from soft to loud.
- She exaggerates consonant sounds, and stretches out vowel sounds.
- She speaks in sentences with few words and simple syntax.
- She leaves pauses in her utterances: she speaks and waits, speaks and waits, as if she were inviting the baby into a conversation and showing him where to slot his utterances.

In short, she is speaking **"Motherese"** (Newport, Gleitman, and Gleitman, 1977).

Motherese reminds you of the way a tennis coach might show a neophyte how to swing a racket. She exaggerates the twisting of the body, the gaze straight ahead toward an unseen opponent, the arm swinging on around after the ball has been hit. So, too, the adult speaking to the child exaggerates the connection of emotion to speech through the dramatic swoops and pauses of her voice, her brightened eyes, and smiling face. Her turn-taking with the child is greatly slowed down, as if to invite the child to take his part in the conversations (Stern, 2004). The mother says "Hey!" and smiles, then waits. Says "Hey!" again and smiles, then waits. Then when the baby finally coos, the mother smiles more brightly, then says "Hey, yourself!" and then waits . . .

As we shall see, adults hold scaffolded conversations with older children, too, that help them learn language. And while Motherese is usually spoken by people unaware that they are doing it, preschool teachers and parents can be trained to use certain kinds of scaffolded conversations with children that help them learn language.

Parents and adults can help children to talk by:

- **Talking to them**, because the more adults talk, the more words and constructions children hear;

- **Talking about things**, because the more we describe things and extend our speech about things, the more names for things and the more kinds of logical structures between ideas children learn;

- **Using rich language**, language that recounts what happened in the past, what will happen if something else takes place, and what we look forward to in the future, because these ways of talking give children a more supple grasp on the way language is used to describe experience and support thinking;

- **Encouraging them**, because the more we encourage children, the more they will say and the more confident and inquisitive they will be.

To the Reader You must pay close attention to this description of children's language development to see how you as a tutor can help children's language expand. The list of suggestions above are useful ones to employ in your tutoring, too. The trick is to find the right balance between stimulating children's interests and responding with language.

Aspects of Language

What do children learn, when they learn language? Although our experience of language is a whole, unitary thing ("We were 'just talking'"), for the sake of understanding what children learn when they learn language, we can focus on five aspects of language that linguists study. They are **phonology**, the sounds of language; **syntax**, the ordering of words and other grammatical bits into meaningful language; **semantics**, or the meaning system of language; and **discourse**, the ways speakers use language in different contexts for different purposes. Before we go, we will address a sixth aspect: **metalinguistic awareness**, the ability to think about language.

Phonology: Making Sense with Sound

Have you ever heard a happy baby babble? Those cheerful, bubbly strings of syllables sound like speech, but they don't mean anything. Here is an odd fact: children at six to ten months babble very nearly all of the speech sounds used in all of the languages in the world. And until she is a year old, unless her caregivers speak Chinese, you cannot tell from her babble what language the baby is being brought up in (Hoff, 2001). At one year, all the sounds drop out of the child's babbling but those of her local language. The baby whose parents speak Kiswahili keeps making "mb-" and "ng-" sounds, but stops making the "-ou-" and "th-" sounds; while the baby in the English-speaking environment does just the opposite. Eventually, the child learns the sound system of her language. That system is called **phonology**, and it has two parts: **phonemes** and **prosody**.

Phonemes   The spoken building blocks of words are called **phonemes**. These are the sounds that roughly correspond to the letters. In the spoken word "dog," for example, the phonemes are the sounds represented by the D, O, and G. In the spoken word "ship," the phonemes are the sounds represented by the SH, I, and P.

Phonemes are "meaningful" sounds—not because they mean anything in themselves, but because they have the power to change the meaning of a word. For example, when we say "chop" and "shop," the first sound in each word tells us that a different word is being spoken. When we say "chop" and "chip," the middle sound signals a difference between words. That means those sounds are different phonemes. In fact, this test of finding "meaningful pairs," two words that are distinguished only by the difference of one phoneme, is the best test of whether or not a sound *is* a phoneme. When you pronounce the P sound in *pit* and *spit* you make a little puff of air in the first case but not the second, as you will see if you hold a piece of paper in front of your mouth. That puff of air is enough to make a difference in words in Arabic, but not in English. In other words, those are two phonemes in Arabic, but only one in English. The same is true of the "sh," "ch," and "j" sounds, and the "t" and "th" sounds in Spanish. They are different phonemes in English, but not in Spanish. That is why Spanish-speaking children may have trouble distinguishing between *choosing your shoes* and *shoesing your choose*.

Prosody   Phonemes aren't the only meaningful sounds in language. The musical qualities of language are also meaningful. Linguists use the generic term **prosody** to refer to three qualities of sound that apply to units larger than the phoneme. Those qualities are **pitch**, **stress**, and **juncture**.

Pitch, of course, refers to how high or low a sound is pronounced. Pitch often conveys meaning. Assume, for example, that your friend tells you, "I have a brother in Alaska." If you say, "Where?" with a rising tone, the friend might say, "In Alaska. Didn't you hear me?" But if you say, "Where?" with a falling tone, your friend might say "Fairbanks," or "Anchorage."

Stress simply means where you place the emphasis within a word or a sentence. Note, for example, how placing the stress on different italicized words signals differences in meaning in these sentences:

My cousin is an American history teacher.

My cousin is an *American* history teacher. (not European history)

My cousin is an American *history* teacher. (not political science)

My *cousin* is an American history teacher. (not my aunt)

Stress makes meaningful differences between single words, too. Note the differences between *con*tract (a document) and con*tract* (to shrink); pro*duce* (to make) and *pro*duce (vegetables from the farm).

Dana Nielson
Preschool Teacher—Geneva Lakefront Child Center

Pronunciation

Even though they learn most of their language from adults, pronunciation is the toughest part of learning language for three-year-olds. They understand what their parent is telling them, but the words come out differently when they try to say the same thing. When I watch my children in their special areas, they tend to role play as the adult. They pretend they are the teacher or a mom or father and talk as though they are the adult. I like to see my children learning to pronounce their words and begin to build their vocabulary while they are in my classroom.

Juncture refers to whether or not syllables are to be considered as joined together in the same word—an important question, because it makes a difference in meaning. Consider the story of the lady from Virginia who moved to New Jersey for a few years. While visiting friends back home in Virginia, she told them people in New Jersey had a puzzling phrase they used when something was expensive: "They say 'It costs *a nominal egg*,'" she reported. Her friends were puzzled, too, until one realized that the New Jerseyites had been saying "It costs *an arm and a leg*."

Teachers rarely teach children prosody. But it is clearly important to children, as witnessed by the case of the fetuses in an experiment whose mothers read them *The Cat in the Hat* for a few weeks before they were born. The fact that the babies could recognize that very book after they were born shows the power of prosody. It must have been the musical qualities of the language that they noticed, since it presumably could not have been the words.

To the Reader Don't memorize these details, but use them to appreciate two things: one is children's accomplishment in learning to talk—it's really quite amazing. The other is the complexity of what children are learning when they are learning language.

Syntax: Helping Words Make Sense

Syntax is a code that speakers use to encode meaning and that hearers use to decode it. Your knowledge of syntax is what enables you to read the sentence, "The farmer bit the cow" and know who was bit and who did the biting. In other words, **syntax** or "grammar" is the set of rules that order words and their inflections into meaningful sentences.

It may surprise you to hear of young children knowing syntax, but indeed they start learning it shortly after they are a year old. They don't know rules of syntax on a conscious level, of course. A preschool child cannot tell you the rule for making nouns plural, but when she says "I got two foots," she is showing you that she knows the pluralization rule on a *tacit level* and can use it. So please get used to this idea: language is orderly. There are hundreds of rules that govern the arrangement of words and their parts to make meaningful sentences—but speakers use these rules unconsciously. Children know hundreds of syntactic rules before they ever enter school.

Syntax works in two ways: through *word order* and *inflectional endings*. In the sentences, "The farmer bit the cow" and "The cow bit the farmer," the order of the words determines the grammatical function of its parts (which one is the do-*er* and which is the do-*ee*), and lets you know who did the biting and who was bitten.

In the two sentences *The farmer bit the cow* and *The farmer bit the cows*, the *inflectional ending -s* on cows tells you that the farmer was on a roll. Inflectional endings can tell you the number of things, how many people are doing an action (*He bites* vs. *They bite*), or whether the action happened in the past or is still going on: (*He hated cows* vs. *He hates cows*).

Children start to learn syntax when they string together two words in a sentence. For most children, this occurs at eighteen to twenty-four months. From then until about the age of four, children gain control over not only inflectional endings such as -*s* and -*ed*, but also the main sentence patterns of their language. By the time they are four years old, most—but not all—children can make statements ("I'm taller than you"), express negative ideas ("You aren't being nice to me"), ask questions ("Why won't the boat go?"), and give commands ("Come here a minute"). They can speak in simple sentences ("I like my skates") compound sentences ("My dog is nice and I love him") and complex sentences ("We're going to eat ice cream when we get home"). Thus, many children are able to say and understand the basic sentence forms of their language by the age of four or five.

But much work remains to be done. First, note that there are some sophisticated constructions that most children still cannot use, like:

- the passive voice ("The cow was bit by the farmer")
- the subjunctive mood ("It's important that she have her work done by noon")
- some conditional tenses ("If the branch hadn't been strong, the bear wouldn't have made it across")

Second, children's syntactic development is limited by the kinds of language the adults around them use (Hart and Risley, 1995). So if the parents don't speak English, or if they speak a truncated version of it, the preschool program will need to be rich in language experiences to expose the child to language she hasn't heard, and to encourage her to practice using richer language.

To the Reader Again, don't get fixated on the details here, but do notice how important this language learning is. Without a well developed knowledge of syntax and phonology (and the other aspects of language that will follow below), children will have only a blurred sense of what other people mean, and their own thinking will be less precise.

But note, too, that the knowledge we are talking about is *tacit knowledge*; that is, you can't teach a child syntax or phonology directly. You must instead engage her in talk, and then be a good language model.

And finally, there are many children who won't understand their teachers or their tutors if they use complex sentence constructions. Preschool teachers report saying "Only when you have finished cutting out the stars should you ask for the glue," and watching some children reach right away for the glue. You should make a habit of examining your own speech to make sure you are expressing yourself in ways that every child understands.

Semantics: Words and Their Meanings

After phonology (the sounds of language) and syntax (the grammar or ordering of language), the third main division of language learning is **semantics**, which is the system of meanings in a language and the way those meanings are encoded in words.

Words   Languages come in units of words, and words have sounds and meanings. They also have nuances, or fine shades of significance, and connotations, or emotional connections. They have social propriety, or manners. Words are close to concepts: they enable speakers to pay attention to things, remember them, and communicate about them with others.

When a community of people shares a language, the words they use point to a collection of all the things those people have found important enough to give names to. We knew an anthropologist who lived on a tiny island in the Pacific where the residents had five different words for "we." Apparently, they needed to distinguish between "the two of us," "this small group gathered around," "our family," "all those within earshot," and "all of us who live on this island." Since many people lived close together, this pronoun made it possible to say "Why don't we have dinner?" without inviting the neighborhood. Words are symbols for the things that have seemed important enough to be carved out of the restless flow of experience, named, recalled, and noticed again. Once a concept has been carved out of experience and named, that part of people's experience is more likely to be noticed in the future (Richards, 1929).

For an individual child, the sum of the words in his vocabulary is closely related to his intelligence. As we said above, a child's vocabulary points in two directions. It is a record of the things she has noticed and thought about, and it is also the set of concepts that will enable her to notice and think about new things in the future. That is why tests of verbal I.Q. are largely measures of vocabulary.

Words and Things   Words vary in their level of generality and specificity. Take a family pet, for example. Her name is her Lucy. She is a springer spaniel, and that is a breed of dog. A dog is a canine—like foxes, wolves, and jackals, but not cats or gerbils. However, canines, cats, and gerbils—but not snakes or lobsters—are all mammals; and all of these, Lucy along with the foxes, gerbils, lobsters, and snakes, are called animals—unlike ferns and pine trees. Yet along with Lucy, foxes, cats, gerbils, lobsters, snakes, ferns, and pine trees are called living things, unlike peat. Still, peat—just like Lucy, the foxes, cats, gerbils, lobsters, snakes, ferns, and pine trees, but not rocks or water—is made of things that used to be alive, so it is called organic matter. So this furry companion you call Lucy is also called a springer spaniel, a dog, a canine, a mammal, an animal, a living thing, and a mass (a lovable mass) of organic matter.

The mental exercise that you just did to locate Lucy in the world of names of things is called *categorization* or *classification*. Teachers know that this sort of activity does not come easily to children. Jean Piaget (1926) observed that most children reach the age of six or seven before they can easily think on all of these levels of generality and specificity at once. To demonstrate Piaget's point, if you ask a four-year-old if she lives in Chicago or Illinois, she is likely to answer one or the other, but not both. Piaget suggests that they cannot think on two levels of a hierarchy at one time. (Many of us find this uncomfortable, too. For instance, consider this: Are we people or mammals?)

Knowledge of the way objects in the world have been classified—that Lucy the family pet is at the same time a springer spaniel, a dog, a canine, a mammal, and an animal—does not come to children through their senses. This is knowledge that has to be learned from older language users—learned by observation and imitation rather than direct teaching, most likely, but learned from others nonetheless. Children need many opportunities to talk meaningfully with fluent language users, while they are immersed in active and interesting situations, so that they will hear words used properly and with proper relations to their referents. In this way they can learn not just words, but the hierarchies of meanings within which the words fit.

How Do Children Learn Vocabulary?   Children vary tremendously in the sizes of their vocabulary. As we saw before, by the age of four or five, the more verbal children will have twice as many words in their vocabularies as their less verbal classmates. By twelfth grade, students with larger vocabularies know four times as many words as their least verbal classmates; and verbal third graders have larger vocabularies than the less verbal twelfth graders (Beck, McKeown, and Kucan, 2002).

Hart and Risley's research (1995) showed that the rate of acquisition of vocabulary among children has widely separated by the time children are three years old, and it continues to widen. The differences in growth rates could be explained almost entirely by the amount and quality of the parents' speech to their children.

Parents who speak a great deal to their children help build vocabulary. Parents who answer children's questions, and ask questions of their own; parents who elaborate on children's ideas; parents who talk about things that have happened, will happen, might happen contingent on something else; parents who encourage and praise—all these parents pass on to their children both a way of describing and a way of understanding experience.

Functions of Language

Now that we have discussed the aspects of phonology, syntax, and semantics, it is time to ask: What are all these things for? That is, how do children do things with language?

The Scottish linguist M.A.K. Halliday (1975) studied what his young, preverbal son Nigel seemed to be trying to do with his unconventional utterances and gestures, and identified the following seven **functions of language** that were obviously present before the child could utter recognizable words or use syntax.

- **The Instrumental Function**—children use utterances and gestures as if they were extensions of their arms, to get things for themselves, such as to be handed something or to be lifted up.

- **The Regulatory Function**—to control other people's behavior, such as to get someone to stop playing with a toy.

- **The Interpersonal Function**—to set up and maintain relationships with other people, as in face-to-face play with a mother, or in teasing (tormenting?) the family dog.

- **The Personal Function**—to express how they are feeling, whether it is joy or loneliness.

- **The Heuristic Function**—to express curiosity and to find things out, such as to discover where an absent parent went or what a noise was.

- **The Imaginative Function**—to play with language and create sounds for one's own and others' enjoyment.

- **The Representational Function**—to communicate knowledge about the world, such as to announce that a guest has arrived.

These seven functions "grow" with the child, and remain the areas of language use in which children continue to develop competence. Thus, even after a child develops a vocabulary of conventional words and a grasp of

Table 2.1   Categories of Language Practice

Language Function	Activity for Practicing That Function
Instrumental	Children make choices and express those choices to the tutor or teacher. At the lunch table, children ask for things politely.
Regulatory	Children follow directions. Children explain to their classmates how to carry out a procedure.
Interpersonal	Children learn to make polite exchanges: "Good morning, Reggie. How are you?" "I'm fine, thank you."
Personal	Children can name the feelings of other children pictured in books. Children begin to describe their own feelings.
Heuristic	Children ask questions about how things work, what will happen next, what something is called.
Imaginative	Children join in on sharing poems, songs, stories, and plays.
Representational	Children report on what the weather is like outside, or what the class did yesterday, or what they did over the weekend.

Source: Adapted from Halliday (1975).

syntax, and after a child begins to learn various verbal strategies to address herself to different audiences, she will continue to add to her skills at using language to get things for herself, to regulate others' behavior, to build relationships, and so on.

You can think of Halliday's functions of language as a kind of menu of language development, and you can arrange activities and circumstances in the preschool room to allow children can use language in all of the ways Halliday named (see Table 2.1).

Milestones in Language Development

Children tend to follow the same pathway to developing language, although, as we have noted, there are large differences from child to child, and these differences are often related to the child's family background. The National Association for the Education of Young Children lists "widely held expectations" for children's language development (see Table 2.2).

Table 2.2 Language and Communication Development:
Widely Held Expectations

For 3-year-olds

- Shows a steady increase in vocabulary, ranging from 2,000 to 4,000 words; tends to over-generalize meaning (that is, to say "dog" for any four-legged animal) and make up words to fit needs (call a motorcycle a "chainsaw bicycle.")
- Uses simple sentences of at least three or four words to express needs
- May have difficulty taking turns in conversation; changes topics quickly
- Pronounces words with difficulty; often mistakes one word for another
- Likes simple finger plays and rhymes and learns words to songs that have much repetition
- Adapts speech and style of non-verbal communication to listeners in culturally accepted ways but still needs to be reminded of context
- Asks who, what, where, and why questions but is confused by some questions (especially why, how, and when)
- Uses language to organize thought, linking two ideas by sentence combining, overuses such words as but, because, and when; rarely makes appropriate use of such temporal words as before, until, or after
- Can tell a simple story but must redo the sequence to put an idea into the order of events; often forgets the point of a story and is most likely to focus on favorite parts

For 4-year-olds

- Expands vocabulary to about 5,000 words; shows more attention to abstract uses
- Usually speaks in five-to-six-word sentences
- Likes to sing simple songs; knows many rhymes and finger plays
- Will talk in front of the group with some reticence; likes to tell others about family and experiences
- Uses verbal commands to claim many things; begins teasing others
- Expresses emotions through facial gestures and reads others for body cues; copies behaviors (such as hand gestures) of older children or adults
- Can control volume of voice for periods of time if reminded; begins to read context for social cues
- Uses more advanced sentence structures, such as relative clauses and tag questions ("She's nice, isn't she?") and experiments with new constructions, creating some comprehension difficulties for the listener
- Tries to communicate more than his or her vocabulary allows; borrows words to create meaning

(continued)

Table 2.2   Continued

- Learns new vocabulary quickly if related to own experience ("We walk our dog on a belt. Oh, it's a leash. We walk our dog on a leash.")
- Can retell a four- or five-step directive or sequence in a story

For 5-year-olds

- Employs a vocabulary of 5,000 to 8,000 words, with frequent plays on words; pronounces words with little difficulty, except for particular sounds, such as "L" and "th"
- Uses fuller, more complex sentences ("His turn is over, and it's my turn now.")
- Takes turns in conversation, interrupts others less frequently; listens to another speaker if information is new and of interest; shows vestiges of egocentrism in speech, for instance, in assuming listener will understand what is meant (saying "He told me to do it" without any antecedents for pronouns)
- Shares experiences verbally; knows the words to many songs
- Likes to act out others' roles, shows off in front of new people or becomes unpredictably very shy
- Remembers lines of simple poems and repeats full sentences and expressions from others, including television shows and commercials
- Shows skills at using conventional modes of communication complete with pitch and inflection
- Uses nonverbal gestures, such as certain facial expressions in teasing peers
- Can tell stories with practice; enjoys repeating stories, poems, and songs; enjoys acting out plays or stories
- Shows growing speech fluency in expressing ideas

Source: Bredekamp and Copple (1997).

Conclusion

Children develop wonderfully in the preschool years. Their language bursts from a one- or two-word "telegraphic" utterance to sentences that ask questions, make statements, and proclaim excitement. Their thinking embraces concepts in logical relationships to each other.

Children in preschool learn much about reading and writing, too. That is the subject of the next chapter.

chapter three

How Does Literacy Emerge?

In what sense can this child be taught to read and write in preschool? In *The Psychology and Pedagogy of Reading*, Edmund Burke Huey argued in 1908 that reading instruction should not start before the age of nine. In most countries of the world, children enter first grade and begin serious reading instruction at the age of six or even seven. What can we teach children about literacy when they are only three or four years old?

A great deal. Since we shifted away from thinking in terms of **reading readiness** and began to research and teach in the new paradigm of **emergent literacy**, educators have realized that an orientation to literacy begins with experiences very early in childhood, even in the first years of life. Early experiences that support literacy include:

- **Learning language**, including a vocabulary rich in names for things, and syntax that supports many kinds of logical relationships among ideas;
- **Hearing stories**, and not only associating delight with them, but also learning to follow their patterns to make meaning;
- **Becoming aware of language**, with its rhythms and rhymes, its words and some of their parts;
- **Getting to know books** and how pictures and texts convey messages;
- **Learning about print**, seeing how it is arrayed on the page, and attending to the features that make letters different from drawings, and that make each letter unique.

Children need these developments in adequate measure to learn how to read, even if their formal reading begins years after early concepts are acquired. Those who work with young children need to understand the concepts and skills that make up emergent literacy. So, read on!

A Language for Literacy

The first and most important component of emergent literacy is a rich base in language. Language and literacy support each other in both directions. From listening to stories read to them, children learn language—an especially rich form of language that we will describe shortly. And having a rich store of language helps children learn to read and write. As linguist Catherine Snow and her colleagues argue,

> Why would anyone seek the sources of success at literacy in the domains of vocabulary or extended discourse skills? Ultimately, reading is a linguistic activity. Of course, there are specifically literate facts and procedures having to do with letters and with sounds they represent that readers need to master. Increasingly, though, evidence suggests that learning about letters and sounds presupposes knowing a lot about the internal structure of words—knowledge that is hard to acquire without first knowing a lot of words. (Snow, et al., 2001, p. 3)

The rich language that supports literacy has four features:

• **It is rich in vocabulary that names things**. The words in books that are read to children are like a palette of labels for concepts. Take, for example, these lines from William Steig's ever-popular children's book, *Sylvester and the Magic Pebble*. The publisher recommends that this book be read to children as young as age four.

> *Sylvester Duncan lived with his mother and father at Acorn Road in Oatsdale. One of his hobbies was collecting pebbles of unusual shape and color.*

The words "hobbies," "collecting," "pebbles," "unusual," and "shape" will be new additions to many young children's vocabulary.

• **It contains a range of syntactical patterns**. The language of books uses present tenses, past tenses, future tenses; it uses complex sentences with *because* . . . statements. These constructions prepare children to learn language that points to different times and to different logical relationships between ideas.

For instance, later in *Sylvester and the Magic Pebble* we read,

> *As he was studying this remarkable pebble, he began to shiver, probably from excitement, and the rain felt cold on his back. "I wish it would stop raining."*
>
> *To his great surprise the stopped. It didn't stop gradually as rains usually do. It CEASED.*

These three sentences express two cause-and-effect relationships: one explains Sylvester's shivering, and the other suggests that Sylvester's wish, aided by the magic pebble, stopped the rain. The third sentence shows an example of a comparison and contrast: the rain CEASED, unlike normal rains, which stop gradually. Sentences containing these kinds of constructions are not often heard in speech—especially not in the speech of families from lower socioeconomic groups.

• **It is organized as extended discourse, often in narrative patterns**. The language of stories is organized into story structures or **story grammars** (Stein, 1975). There is a **character** (think Sylvester) in a **setting** (Oatsdale!) who has a **problem** (Sylvester, to escape being eaten by lions, accidentally wishes to turn into a stone, does do through the magic of the pebble, and can't resume his former shape). There are several **attempts** (the efforts of the many people searching for Sylvester) to find a **solution** to the problem (his parents' picking up the pebble and wishing Sylvester's return), and there is a **consequence** of the actions: a state of affairs at the end that is

Linda Kucan
Assistant Professor—Appalachian State University

Types of Language Interactions

Children are eager to discover and use words, words to wrap around people and animals, objects and places, feelings and ideas. For young children, oral language interactions are opportunities for learning words. In robust verbal encounters, children hear interesting and precise words used by adults, and they are encouraged to notice, ask about, and use such words themselves. Children are also invited to play with words through rhyming and comparing and even making up new ones—like Dr. Seuss!

different from the beginning (Sylvester lives cozily with his family and never again dabbles in magic). Children who are read to learn the grammar of stories, and having this grammar enables them to comprehend other stories more successfully.

• **It is decontextualized**. In everyday speech, when we say "Stop that!" or "What's this?" there is a "that" or a "this" that supports the meaning of the words. But the language of books points to things that are remote from us. For instance, from the first lines of *Sylvester*, the young listeners are asked to imagine a setting in which animals wear clothes and behave like middle-class people. The setting has to be invented in the listeners' imaginations, using the suggestions from the words. We call this sort of language use *decontextualized*. Children learn to appreciate decontextualized language through much early experience with it; without it, they may find their first experiences with literature to be a little disorienting.

As you can see, as a tutor you can help a child gain the language base for literacy by talking with them, reading to them, and engaging them in fantasy play.

Language Awareness

People pledge love, declare war, or forecast blizzards without being conscious of the language they use to do these things. But children learning to read have to be conscious of language. Because print represents spoken language, emergent readers need to be aware of the **words** out of which language is built. They also need to be aware of the **sounds**. If their language is Japanese, the sounds are at the level of syllables. But if their language is an alphabetic one like English (and Spanish, French, and Kiswahili), readers must be aware of sounds at the level of **onsets and rimes**, and **phonemes**. True, a full awareness of language does not usually develop in preschool children, but the early experiences that lead to language awareness occur there—or they don't. That is why teachers and tutors, too, need to be aware of what we mean by language awareness.

The Concept of Word

The first unit of language of which young readers need to be aware is the word. Distinguishing words in speech is not a simple matter, because speech usually comes to us all run together. We more often hear someone say "Whuzapnin?" than "What is happening?" Once children are aware that language comes in word units, they can "track along" with print, by matching the words in their minds with the words on the page.

Most children begin to develop a solid concept of word in later kindergarten and early first grade (Morris and Slavin, 2002). But it helps if they have early experiences that call attention to individual words—especially since this can be done playfully and naturally (see below).

Not being aware of words in speech puts children at a disadvantage when they are learning to read. Suppose a teacher teaches the children the song "The Corner Grocery Store" and writes the words on chart paper. The teacher then asks the children to look at the printed words as they sing them from memory. A child who is aware of word units—who has a **concept of word**—can look at the word "corner" at just the instant she sings it. A child who does not have the concept of word may scan her eyes across a whole line of text as she sings the word "corner." Or she may look at only a single letter. In either case, at the conclusion of the activity, a child who lacks the concept of word is unlikely to have learned to recognize any new words from it. The child who had the concept of word, who looked at the written words just at the instant she sang each word, will have been in a position to associate the written version of the words with the spoken versions, and is likely to learn to read several of them from the activity.

Later in this chapter, we describe ways to help emergent readers develop a concept of word.

Phonological Awareness

When we speak of phonological awareness, we mean that the child is aware of the sounds in language and can respond to those sounds in some way. It will help a child learn to read later on if she is aware of *syllables, onsets and rimes*, and *phonemes*.

Syllables These are the "pulses" of language. They are the "beats" we hear in **elbow** (two syllables), **love** (one syllable), and **popsicle** (three syllables).

Because syllables are easy to clap along to, four-year-old children can begin to sense them. When they do, they are beginning to track along with speech sounds, which is a beginning level of language awareness that will prepare them to make future gains.

Onsets and Rimes Below the level of the syllable, we can separate the first part of the syllable from the part that follows. The **onset** is the beginning consonant sound in a syllable (if the syllable has one), and the **rime** is the vowel sound plus any consonant sound that follows. In "cat," for instance, the onset is /**k**/ and the rime is –**at**. In "step" the onset is **st** and the rime is -**ep**. By late kindergarten or early first grade, many children are aware that syllables can be broken down into these two parts. Before that, four-year-olds enjoy playing with rhyming words—good practice that will prepare them to become more aware of onsets and rimes later.

Being aware of onsets and rimes is important to emergent readers, because it enables them to think of words in families, and to learn to read several words once they learn to read just one. For example, the child who can read **cat** can easily learn to read **sat, fat, rat**, and **mat**, if she is aware of onsets and rimes and knows the sounds of those consonants. Most four-year-old children are still unable to make these distinctions, but they do enjoy jump-rope rhymes and songs, and by using rhyming language, they are preparing themselves to break words into onsets and rimes when they are older.

Phonemes We can break syllables down still further into the smallest constituents of sound, the **phonemes**. Phonemes roughly correspond to letters. For example, **dig** has three phonemes: /d/, /i/, and /g/. **Clam** has four phonemes: /k/, /l/, /æ/, and /m/. Because alphabetic languages like English are written by making matches between letters and phonemes, it is necessary for beginning readers to have some ability to hear the separate phonemes in a word (Adams, 1991; and Snow, et al., 1998). The memory storage for words is improved if readers are aware of their phonemes (Ehri, 1989). Thus, if a young reader is aware of phonemes, she will have an advantage when it comes to storing up a repertoire of words she can read instantaneously.

Both of these events—learning to read words and remembering them—are far into the future when a child is four years old. But word play that calls attention to individual speech sounds is good practice for getting there.

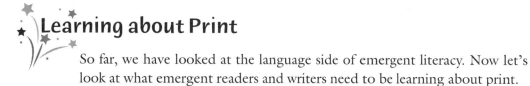

To the Reader Here we go trotting out one detailed notion after another: *concept of word, onsets and rimes, phonemes*—"Is it *necessary* to talk of such things?" Yep. You would be amazed to know how much attention has been paid to these matters among literacy experts. It literally took an act of Congress—no joke—to identify the key components of early literacy—the key ingredients that some children were missing that made them likely to fail to learn to read later (Snow, et al., 1998). So far, these are what the consensus of the experts have identified as the key skills children need to start developing in preschool, so they can become competent readers later.

Learning about Print

So far, we have looked at the language side of emergent literacy. Now let's look at what emergent readers and writers need to be learning about print.

Concepts about Print

When teachers face a group of young kindergarten learners in a reading lesson, they make certain assumptions about what the children already know. As the New Zealand researcher Marie Clay demonstrates in the following piece, sometimes those assumptions are wrong:

Suppose the teacher has placed an attractive picture on the wall and has asked her children for a story, which she will record under it. They offer the text, "Mother is cooking," which the teacher alters slightly to introduce some features she wishes to teach. She writes:

Mother said, "I am baking."

If she says, "Now look at our *story*, 30% of the new entrant group [children who are just beginning reading instruction] will attend to the *picture*. If she says, "Look at the words and find some that you know," between 50 and 90% will be looking for *letters*. If she says, "Can you see Mother, most will agree that they can, but some *see* her in the picture, some can locate *M*, and others will locate the word *Mother*.

Perhaps the children read in unison, "Mother is . . ." and the teacher tries to sort this out. Pointing to *said*, she asks, "Does this say *is*?" Half agree that it does because it has *s* in it. "What letter does it start with?" Now the teacher is really in trouble. She assumes that the children will *know* that a word is built out of letters, but 50% of the children still confuse the verbal labels *word* and *letter* after six months of instruction. She also assumes that the children know that the left-hand letter following a space is the "start" of a word. Often they do not. (Clay, 1975, pp. 3–4)

As Clay's example demonstrates, for a reading lesson to work for a child, there are *concepts about print* that she must have in place so that she can orient herself properly to a book and direct her attention appropriately to the units of words and letters.

Teachers and tutors often do not teach explicit reading lessons to four-year-olds, but they strive to give children experience with books and an orientation to print. An orientation to print typically builds concepts like the following:

- *Knowledge of the layout of books.* The child should know that we read the book from front to back. She should know what the cover of the book is. When handed a book to read, she should be able to hold the book right side up and open it from the front.

- *Knowledge that print, not pictures, is what we read.* If shown a spread with both print and a picture, the child should realize that the print and not the picture is where the words are written, and should be able to "point to the part where we read."

- *Directional orientation of print on the page.* The child should know that the printed text runs from left to right, returns to the left, and proceeds toward the bottom, and should be able to "Show where we begin reading. Show where we go after that. Show where we go after that."

- *Know the terms, "top," "bottom," "beginning," "end," "first," and "last" with respect to the text on a page.* When the teacher is talking about the top and the bottom of the page, the beginning and end of the sentence, and the first and last page, the child should be able to indicate what parts of the text are referred to by pointing to them.

- *Understand the terms "word" and "letter."* The child should know what the terms "letter" and "word" refer to by pointing to them.

More advanced children may be able to demonstrate the following:

- *Recognize uppercase and lowercase letters.* If the teacher points to an uppercase letter **A**, can the child point to a lowercase letter **a** on the same page?

- *Know punctuation.* Some children know that a period means we should stop, a question mark means we are asking a question, and an exclamation point signals something exciting or important. (After Clay, 2000)

Linda Kucan
Assistant Professor—Appalachian State University

Books and the Power of Words

Reading books and talking about them is a powerful context for developing an awareness of and appreciation for the power of words to evoke cognitive and affective responses. Research has shown that such interactions are vital if children are to build a foundation for literacy. By the time children enter kindergarten, there are dramatic differences in oral language and vocabulary development between those who have participated in thoughtful and enjoyable conversations and read-aloud sessions with caregivers and educators, and those who have had only limited exposure to such experiences. The gap only widens as children progress through school. It is vital that all those who care about children and their growth in literacy make oral language and vocabulary development a priority.

Graphic Principles

What about scribbles? Give a child a marker or a crayon and he will scribble. If he has looked closely at books and has watched others writing, his scribbles will look a little bit like print. In fact, many four-year-olds make scribbles that deserve to be called **mock** writing, because it appears that children are trying to imitate adult writing. Here, for example, is mock writing produced by children whose families write in Arabic, Hebrew, and English. Amazingly, although none of the marks are legitimate graphemes in any of the languages, each piece shares features with the family's writing system (see Figure 3.1).

Figure 3.1   Children's Scribbles Approximate Their Respective Writing Systems

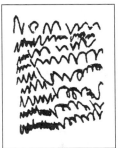

Dawn, a 4-year-old from the United States, writes in unconventional script using a series of wavy lines. Each line is written from left-to-right. Dawn creates a page of such lines starting at the top of her page and finishing at the bottom of her page.

Najeeba, a 4-year-old from Saudi Arabia, writes in unconventional script using a series of very intricate curlicue formations with lots of "dots" over the script. When she completes her story she says, "Here, but you can't read it, cause I wrote it in Arabic and in Arabic we use a lot more dots than you do in English!"

Ofer, a 4-year-old from Israel, prints, first right-to-left, then left-to-right, using a series of rectangular and triangular shapes to create his story, which his grandmother says, ". . . looks like Hebrew, but it's not." Her concern because he sometimes writes "backwards" sounds like the concerns of many parents and teachers in the U.S., with the difference being that left-to-right is "backwards" in Hebrew, and right-to-left "backwards" in English.

Source: Woodward, Harste, and Burke (1994).

What, then, are some graphic features of English writing that children display in their mock writing? The following set of graphic principles was identified by Marie Clay (1975).

The Recurring Principle   Maybe the most basic feature of writing is that writers make the same kind of mark over and over again, usually in a line, to fill a page—unlike drawing, where marks of different kinds are arranged two-dimensionally. A young child's mock writing is often composed of the same mark, roughly the same size, repeated again and again, in a linear arrangement (see Figure 3.2). Children whose language is English will sometimes show a preference for linked and continuous marks that resemble cursive writing, or discrete marks that resemble print.

Figure 3.2   The Recurring Principle

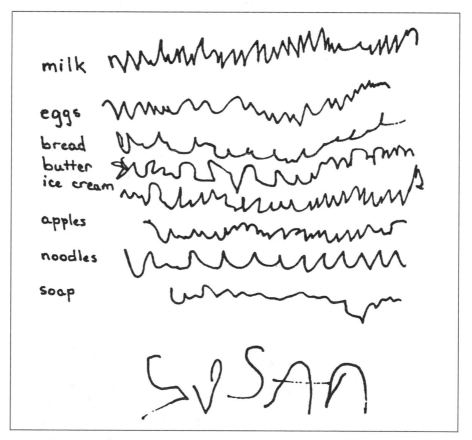

Source: Temple, Nathan, Burris, and Temple (1993).

The Generative Principle   The *generative principle* is the idea that a few marks or characters can be combined and recombined in different orders to produce a whole page or more of writing. We see children taking advantage of the generative principle when they have learned to write a few letters, such as those that spell their own name. Then they combine and recombine those letters to generate many lines of text (see Figure 3.3).

The generative principle, of course, is real. It is a key advantage to alphabetic writing. Whereas speakers of Chinese must learn to write and read some 6,000 characters by the time they finish grade school, speakers of English need only 26 letters (52, counting the uppercase ones) to write all of the words in *Webster's Unabridged Dictionary*. Don't be surprised to hear a child who has generated a page of mock writing show it to you and ask, "What did I write?" As Marie Clay (1975) observed in her book by that title, children at this stage feel that they can now generate writing—but because they cannot yet read, they rely on the adults around them to tell them what their creations mean!

The Flexibility Principle   The flexibility principle has two parts. One part is the idea that a letter you know how to write may be made slightly differently and still be the same letter. For example, a child can write the letter **A** large or small, leaning forward or leaning backward, and it will still be the letter **A**. But a young child doesn't know exactly which variations are allowable for the same letter, and which turn it into a different letter, or nothing at all. That leads to the other part of the flexibility principle.

Figure 3.3   The Generative Principle

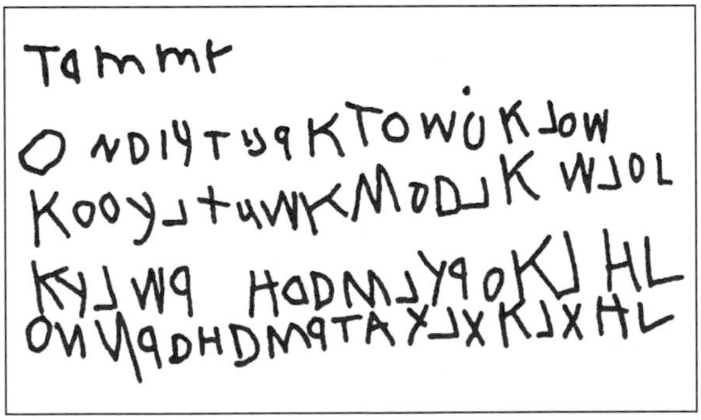

Tommr
O NDIYTY9KTOWUKJOW
KOOYJ+uWKMODJK WJOL
KJJW9 HODMJY9OKJ HL
ONV9DHDM9TAXJJXKJXHL

Source: Temple, Nathan, Burris, and Temple (1993).

Figure 3.4   The Flexibility Principle

Source: Temple, Nathan, Burris, and Temple (1993).

That is, the letter you know how to write may be altered to give you a letter you didn't know how to write. For example, the letter **L** is made from a vertical bar with one horizontal bar. If the child adds a horizontal bar, she makes an **F**. If she adds two horizontal bars, she makes an **E**. What happens if she adds four horizontal bars? Or five? If the child does not yet know the whole repertoire of letters (the alphabet), she might have some luck creating more letters by varying the ones she knows (see Figure 3.4).

Directional Principles   Directional principles have to do with learning to associate the identity of letters with the directions they face. Letters are nearly the only things in children's experience whose identity changes with their orientation in space, so it is not surprising that children find it hard to remember in what direction a letter should be oriented. What is surprising, from an adult point of view, is how easily children can shift from one direction to another when they write. As we see in Figure 3.5, a six-year-old child who starts writing on the right hand side of the page may find it natural to reverse the letters and write a whole line of text from right to left.

Figure 3.5   Directional Problems in Writing

Source: Temple, Nathan, Burris, and Temple (1993).

In past years, children's tendency to reverse letters was taken as a sign of a dysfunctional brain, but now we see it as a sign of immaturity and inexperience with print. Reversing letters and whole lines of print is natural to young children who are learning the directionality principle (Temple, Nathan, Burris, and Temple, 1993).

In summary, scribbling—or mock writing—is a good thing! A child who scribbles

- Is exploring the nature of print, and seeking to discover its distinctive features
- Is showing you, the teacher, what he has discovered so far about the writing system.

To the Reader It can be fascinating to look at children's scribbles and examine them for features of print that the child is trying to use. And of course, you will need to encourage the children to produce written messages. For example, you can invite them to write grocery lists, thank-you notes, and parking tickets—although of course they will be using mock writing.

Alphabet Knowledge

Children who are learning to read and write will need to know several letters of the alphabet. However, they don't need to know them before they make more global discoveries about how reading and writing work, or about the nature of print. Typically, children produce mock writing and do pretend reading (see the next section) before their attention goes to the detail of letters.

Most children can recognize and produce some letters while in preschool, but many still do not. Kindergarten teachers treat children's alphabet knowledge as a sign that they have been exposed to print (Walsh, et al., 1988). They also realize that the more letters children know, the more quickly they will learn to read words (Snow, et al., 1998; Morris, 1999). It's a good idea to take every natural opportunity to teach children about letters. For example, you can label their cubby with their name, and point out, "This is Takisha's cubby because her name starts with T." You can bake alphabet cookies, and serve alphabet soup—making a point, and often a game, of naming the letters as you do.

Invented Spelling

At some point in children's attempts at producing writing, **invented spelling** appears. Invented spelling is the attempt to use letters or letter-like strings to convey messages. In a way that is analogous to the process of learning to talk, children who write with invented spelling

- Are trying to discover how the writing system works
- Invent their own ways to use writing to communicate messages
- Go through stages as their own efforts approximate more and more closely the ways that adults write.

Below we will sketch the stages through which children's spelling seems to grow. They are the *prephonemic stage,* the *early phonemic stage,* the *letter-name stage,* and the *transitional stage.* They are followed by a *correct stage.* Preschool children, if they use writing communicatively at all, normally produce writing in the first two or three stages.

Prephonemic Stage of Spelling   Prephonemic spelling is made by children who have seen writing around them and want to produce some of their own. A child doing this kind of spelling uses letters without regard to their sounds, so it is not true spelling. Because not much judgment goes into which letters to write where, children who spell at the prephonemic stage often fill whole pages with letters. As mentioned earlier, don't be surprised if the child then shows you the page and asks, "What did I write?" After all, she knows you know how to read, and she doesn't. If you say, "Xplatwpolcxzahe!" the child will surely howl with glee and dash off to write more.

The child at the prephonemic stage of spelling knows how to make many of the letters, and she also makes many more pseudo-letters—after all, she doesn't know the complete set, so she is not sure what kind of squiggle is a letter and what isn't (see Figure 3.6).

Figure 3.6   Prephonemic Spelling

Source: Temple, Nathan, Burris, and Temple (1993).

Spelling at the Early Phonemic Stage   *Early phonemic* spellers are just beginning to represent words by their phonemes. They usually write a lot less, because they are having to figure out phoneme by phoneme how to spell what they want to say. The breakthrough is that these young writers have discovered the **alphabetic principle**—the idea that we spell words by using letters to represent phonemes. But their drawback is that their concept of word (see above) is not very strong yet. They can't make spoken words "hold still in their minds" while they pull them apart and match letters with their sounds. So they spell only some of the sounds in words, and typically represent only the first and last and possibly a middle consonant, and leave out vowels, like the child who wrote the sample in Figure 3.7.

Spelling at the Letter-Name Stage   A four-year-old child wrote the label to the picture in Figure 3.8. We call this the *letter-name stage* of spelling. This child represented all or nearly all of the phonemes in a word, but he did so by discovering those relationships: nobody *taught* her to spell like that!

But wait: she made logical judgments when choosing letters to represent sounds, but it was the kind of logic that most young spellers use. Let's

Figure 3.7   Early Phonemic Spelling

Figure 3.8   Letter-Name Stage of Spelling

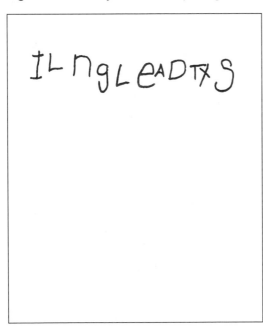

Source: Temple, Nathan, Burris, and Temple (1993).   *Source:* Temple, Nathan, Burris, and Temple (1993).

Charles Temple
Professor of Education—Hobart and William Smith Colleges

Invented Spelling

To appreciate what children are doing with invented spelling, you need something of a trained eye. It's true. Children must have been doing invented spelling since writing was invented, yet we can pinpoint the time—right around 1970—when adults first noticed it. That was when Carol Chomsky and Charles Read, both sophisticated students of linguistics, asked preschool children to write captions to pictures and examined the results. Today, we know that children enjoy representing messages with written marks, and that doing so is good for them. It helps them learn to write and it helps them learn to read, because it motivates them to examine the relations between marks on the page and the language they speak.

look closely at that logic, which is called the *letter-name strategy* (Read, 1975). Children who are letter-name spellers sense the alphabetic principle, and they expect letters to represent the smallest sounds in words, the phonemes. The trouble is, they still have not had enough experience with reading to know how the letters actually represent sounds, so they use letters by their names, as if the names were "building blocks" of sound. They spell as if the idea were to match the sound in the letter's name to the phoneme they want to represent. Sometimes this "letter-name strategy" leads them to write words that look reasonable, and other times they look bizarre.

Let's take a close look at the writing in Figure 3.8. Many consonant sounds are spelled in ways that look reasonable, such as the spellings of F, L, and P in FLEPR (*Flipper*), and of D in AD *(and)*. That's because the names of these letters sound pretty much like the phonemes they're used to represent.

Now here comes the tricky part. The spelling of Y for the /w/ sound in YUTS (*once*) and YET *(went)*, looks odd. Here the child did the same thing he did with the letters F, L, and P, though. To the child's way of thinking, the letter name for W ("double U") doesn't sound at all like /w/, while the name of Y ("wye") is close, so writing Y for the /w/ sound is the logical choice for the child who is using the letter-name strategy.

Linguists use the term *digraphs* to name single phonemes that are spelled with two letters. English has several, such as TH, SH, and CH, and

TCH. Children don't realize that by a convention, two letters represent one sound, so they look for a single letter name that sounds closest to the sound they want to spell. In Figure 3.8, the child used the single letter H to spell the SH digraph in FEHEG (*fishing*) and HE (*she*). She probably did this because, first, she assumed that one sound is spelled by one letter, and second, because the name of the one letter that sounds closest to the phoneme /sh/ is H. (It won't be surprising if this logic isn't obvious to you: you've known how to spell correctly for too long!)

We could say more about these things, but that much should be enough to show that children can be amazingly insightful and creative as they try to figure out how the writing system works. And they should be encouraged to keep exploring. Research shows that the practice of invented spelling is good for young children. Children who are encouraged to invent spellings learn to recognize more words than children who don't use invented spelling. Teachers are advised not to make a fetish out of invented spelling, though. Children like to be taught to write some words correctly, too. And it is good practice to have them read materials that are written correctly, when they are learning how to read.

Language and Print Together: The Development of Storybook Reading

We have looked so far at mock writing. What about mock reading?

When we read a riveting storybook to children who are age three or four, they often ask us to read it again. What happens if we ask the child to read that favorite storybook back to us? With a little encouragement, most children will pretend-read the book, and when they do, they are demonstrating for us their conception of what reading is. Sulzby (1985) has documented stages or advancing strategies that young children use when they are pretend-reading storybooks. Here they are, from simplest to most advanced.

Picture Naming   In the earliest of the book-reading strategies, the child points at the picture, shouts the name of the depicted object, then points to the next page and does the same thing. As Sulzby notes, such a child is repeating a ritual she has been through many times with a parent or other adult reader, who often opens a book, points to a picture, says, "What's that?" waits for the child's answer, then says, "Right! That's a _____!"

Verbal Storytelling, with Conversation   Slightly later, sometime around the age of four or five, the child will point to the pictures and then weave an oral story around them, in a conversation with the adult. This isn't a stand-alone story yet; it still relies on an adult for support. And it is cued by the pictures, rather than by the print on the page or the exact words the child remembers from the adult's reading.

Verbal Storytelling, without Conversation   At a slightly later time, often in his fifth year, a child will now tell a story as he pages through the book from picture to picture. The story is clearly a *told* story, and if he pretend-reads this book more than once, he will make no attempt to keep the wording the same.

Talking Like a Book   Still later, the child will take on a sing-song, rather distant voice that sounds like a reader—sometimes even complete with stumbling over words—as she creates a monologue to accompany the pictures. Amazingly, she is still not actually reading the words—if you look over her shoulder you will see that her monologue bears little resemblance to what is on the page.

Refusal to Read   At a still later stage, when asked to read the book aloud to us, the child will become troubled by the request and tell us she can't. Why? Because she doesn't know how to read the words. This is actually a breakthrough. Not knowing the words didn't keep her from pretend-reading the book before. But now she seems to have realized that in order to read a book, you have to look at the print and know how to pronounce it as spoken language.

Reading a Word or Two   Still later, when you ask the child to pretend-read the book to you, she will look for words she knows and read them aloud.

   This fascinating sequence of strategies shows the child moving from a series of isolated verbal responses to pictures, to a woven verbal text—first with the support of conversation, and then without support, followed by a phase of talking like a book, and then leading to the realization that in order to really read, one must know how to bring to life exactly the words that are written on the page. Once that last discovery is made, the child is ready to match the words she expects with the words on the page (and, doubtless bringing into play other knowledge of print, such as the concept of word

Rebecca Yochelson
Jumpstart Corps Member—Geneva, NY
"Children who are read to at an early age develop their vocabulary and learn to use their imagination. Reading is also a productive way to spend one-on-one time with a child, which is essential in early development."

and knowledge of letters) and read a few words aloud. She has gone from playful imitation of the whole of reading to a careful study of the details. Bit by bit, and especially if she is given books written on an accessible level, she will be able to return to the whole, as she reads the whole book aloud—even if that moment comes after she has left your preschool center.

To the Reader   The last two sections are worth reading twice. They show that children who appear to be fooling around, pretending to write with scribbles and pretending to read books may actually be learning the features of what writing and reading are and how to do them. Now, if your implicit theory of how children read and write said that children had to be taught the letters of the alphabet, and then learn to make words and then learn to read them, you might have missed the actual literacy learning that was going on right in front of you, as you invited children to draw pictures and write messages underneath them, and as you read children a storybook and then invited them to read it back to you.

Benchmarks in Emergent Literacy

So much has been learned about emergent literacy in recent years that we are able to chart with some confidence children's growth toward literacy before they can conventionally read or write a single word. The National Association for the Education of Young Children and the International Reading Association have agreed on the set of benchmarks for emergent literacy growth that are presented in the box on page 65.

Benchmarks of Emergent Literacy

Learning to Read and Write: Developmentally Appropriate Practices for Young Children, Part 4: Continuum of Children's Development in Early Reading and Writing

A joint position of the International Reading Association (IRA) and the National Association for the Education of Young Children (NAEYC)

[Note: this list is intended to be illustrative, not exhaustive. Children at any grade level will function at a variety of phases along the reading/writing continuum.]

Phase 1: Awareness and exploration (goals for preschool)

Children explore their environment and build the foundations for learning to read and write.

Children can
- enjoy listening to and discussing storybooks
- understand that print carries a message
- engage in reading and writing attempts
- identify labels and signs in their environment
- participate in rhyming games
- identify some letters and make some letter-sound matches
- use known letters or approximations of letters to represent written language (especially meaningful words like their name and phrases such as "I love you")

What teachers do
- share books with children, including Big Books, and model reading behaviors
- talk about letters by name and sounds
- establish a literacy-rich environment
- reread favorite stories
- engage children in language games
- promote literacy-related play activities
- encourage children to experiment with writing

What parents and family members can do
- talk with children, engage them in conversation, give names of things, show interest in what a child says
- read and reread stories with predictable text to children

(continued)

- encourage children to recount experiences and describe ideas and events that are important to them
- visit the library regularly
- provide opportunities for children to draw and print, using markers, crayons, and pencils

Phase 2: Experimental reading and writing (goals for kindergarten)

Children develop basic concepts of print and begin to engage in and experiment with reading and writing.

Kindergartners can
- enjoy being read to and themselves retell simple narrative stories or informational texts
- use descriptive language to explain and explore
- recognize letters and letter-sound matches
- show familiarity with rhyming and beginning sounds
- understand left-to-right and top-to-bottom orientation and familiar concepts of print
- match spoken words with written ones
- begin to write letters of the alphabet and some high-frequency words

What teachers do
- encourage children to talk about reading and writing experiences
- provide many opportunities for children to explore and identify sound-symbol relationships in meaningful contexts
- help children to segment spoken words into individual sounds and blend the sounds into whole words (for example, by slowly writing a word and saying its sound)
- frequently read interesting and conceptually rich stories to children
- provide daily opportunities for children to write
- help children build a sight vocabulary
- create a literacy-rich environment for children to engage independently in reading and writing

What parents and family members can do
- daily read and reread narrative and informational stories to children
- encourage children's attempts at reading and writing
- allow children to participate in activities that involve writing and reading (for example, cooking, making grocery lists)
- play games that involve specific directions (such as "Simon Says")
- have conversations with children during mealtimes and throughout the day

Phase 3: Early reading and writing (goals for first grade)

Children begin to read simple stories and can write about a topic that is meaningful to them.

First-graders can

- read and retell familiar stories
- use strategies (rereading, predicting, questioning, contextualizing) when comprehension breaks down
- use reading and writing for various purposes on their own initiative
- orally read with reasonable fluency
- use letter-sound associations, word parts, and context to identify new words
- identify an increasing number of words by sight
- sound out and represent all substantial sounds in spelling a word
- write about topics that are personally meaningful
- attempt to use some punctuation and capitalization

What teachers do

- support the development of vocabulary by reading daily to the children, transcribing their language, and selecting materials that expand children's knowledge and language development
- model strategies and provide practice for identifying unknown words
- give children opportunities for independent reading and writing practice
- read, write, and discuss a range of different text types (poems, informational books)
- introduce new words and teach strategies for learning to spell new words
- demonstrate and model strategies to use when comprehension breaks down
- help children build lists of commonly used words from their writing and reading

What parents and family members can do

- talk about favorite storybooks
- read to children and encourage them to read to you
- suggest that children write to friends and relatives
- bring to a parent-teacher conference evidence of what your child can do in writing and reading
- encourage children to share what they have learned about their writing and reading

(continued)

Phase 4: Transitional reading and writing (goals for second grade)

Children begin to read more fluently and write various text forms using simple and more complex sentences.

Second-graders can

- read with greater fluency
- use strategies more efficiently (rereading, questioning, and so on) when comprehension breaks down
- use word identification strategies with greater facility to unlock unknown words
- identify an increasing number of words by sight
- write about a range of topics to suit different audiences
- use common letter patterns and critical features to spell words
- punctuate simple sentences correctly and proofread their own work
- spend time reading daily and use reading to research topics

What teachers do

- create a climate that fosters analytic, evaluative, and reflective thinking
- teach children to write in multiple forms (stories, information, poems)
- ensure that children read a range of texts for a variety of purposes
- teach revising, editing, and proofreading skills
- teach strategies for spelling new and difficult words
- model enjoyment of reading

What parents and family members can do

- continue to read to children and encourage them to read to you
- engage children in activities that require reading and writing
- become involved in school activities
- show children your interest in their learning by displaying their written work
- visit the library regularly
- support your child's specific hobby or interest with reading materials and references

Phase 5: Independent and productive reading and writing (goals for third grade)

Children continue to extend and refine their reading and writing to suit varying purposes and audiences.

Third-graders can

- read fluently and enjoy reading
- use a range of strategies when drawing meaning from the text

- use word identification strategies appropriately and automatically when encountering unknown words
- recognize and discuss elements of different text structures
- make critical connections between texts
- write expressively in many different forms (stories, poems, reports)
- use a rich variety of vocabulary and sentences appropriate to text forms
- revise and edit their own writing during and after composing
- spell words correctly in final writing drafts

What teachers do

- provide opportunities daily for children to read, examine, and critically evaluate narrative and expository texts
- continue to create a climate that fosters critical reading and personal response
- teach children to examine ideas in texts
- encourage children to use writing as a tool for thinking and learning
- extend children's knowledge of the correct use of writing conventions
- emphasize the importance of correct spelling in finished written products
- create a climate that engages all children as a community of literacy learners

What parents and family members can do

- continue to support children's learning and interest by visiting the library and bookstores with them
- find ways to highlight children's progress in reading and writing
- stay in regular contact with your child's teachers about activities and progress in reading and writing
- encourage children to use and enjoy print for many purposes (such as recipes, directions, games, and sports)
- build a love of language in all its forms and engage children in conversation

This document is an official position statement of the International Reading Association and the National Association for the Education of Young Children

Note that these benchmarks provide a way to track children's progress toward emergent literacy. But in truth, many children lag behind where they should be in emergent literacy development. For these children, the benchmarks can point the way toward the experiences we want to provide to stimulate development in the areas that need growth.

Conclusion

Preschool teachers and volunteer tutors are in the enviable position of seeing the emergence of the really fascinating concepts we have described in this chapter. They can have confidence that children's creativity and exploration are supported, they will continue to make discoveries about the way our language and writing system work, and they will one day become strong readers.

chapter four

How Do We Help Language and Literacy Emerge?

Tutors are well placed to help children grow their language, and to nudge them to get ideas about literacy that will make it easier to learn to read and write later on. The one-on-one attention you can give is price-less to children. But, of course, you need to know what to do. Helping children develop language and literacy is not a matter of sitting them down and teaching them something. So what is it? What do you need to do in order to help? In this chapter, we will suggest some general strategies and some specific activities.

First, let's get our priorities straight. In this chapter, we will suggest that tutors work on developing children's language and developing their emergent literacy concepts. Let's look first at language.

To the Reader This chapter is sort of the pay-off for everything that has been presented already in this book. Chapter One showed you why early literacy intervention is so important for those who need it. Chapter Two helped inform your working theory of how children learn to think and talk, and Chapter Three showed literacy development in some detail. Now we will present ideas to inform your teaching. This part isn't a recipe book. You will still need to use your informed judgment about the ways children learn, and let the methods suggested in this chapter spur you to invent methods of your own, and to be receptive to other good ideas where you find them.

Talking for Vocabulary Development

You can't teach language through so many explicit lessons. Language ability is sunk too deep for that. But you can take the language children offer and help it grow. Doing the things described in the following sections will help.

"Follow in Order to Lead"

For a child to learn a word or a phrase, three things must happen at the same time:

1. The child must be paying attention to something.

2. He must want to communicate about it.

3. He must have an example of the new word or phrase available, usually provided by an adult speaker (Shaffer, 2004; Vygotsky, 1986).

Dick Allington
Vice President—International Reading Association

One-Size-Fits-All Lessons

No child needs to be left behind, but I worry that too many will be as the result of pressures to use one-size-fits-all lessons. We know a lot about how to support and accelerate the development of children who are "behind." Now we must convince policymakers and school administrators to provide those children with the sorts of rich learning opportunities that will move them along and help them become readers and writers. But such lessons are not easily packaged because children differ. Because of that, children who struggle to learn to read respond best to more personalized teaching that provides rich and extended opportunities to read and write.

This means that as tutors, we often "follow in order to lead." That is, we watch carefully and tune into what the child is paying attention to. We name the thing, ask questions about it, and expand on the child's utterance. And we keep it real—children are turned off by language interactions that are too didactic, that are more focused on teaching than they are on the events of the moment.

For example, if the child is opening a wooden box, we might say:

Tutor: "Hey, can you really get the top to open? What do you think you will find inside? Do you think it will be a diamond ring? A pirate's treasure? A ticket to the movies?"

When the child responds, we treat his utterance with respect:

Child: "Ticket."

Tutor: "A ticket, eh. I hope so. A ticket is small enough to fit in the box. But so is a, a—diamond ring. I'm hoping there's a diamond ring in that box. It's small enough to fit in there, too. But could anything else fit in there?"

Child: "Money...."

Use Science Talk/Object Talk

Children's curiosity is stimulated by interesting things we put in their way. So we set up a craft or science activity, we cook something together, or we bring a box turtle, a gerbil, or a colorful picture. We talk about the features we see, and ask the child to comment, too. Again we:

- **Comment**,

- **Question**,

- **Gently encourage the child's talk** by taking it seriously and asking for more, and

- **Expand her utterance** with well-chosen words in our own comments.

For example, children in one Jumpstart site love to make "Magic Mud," a concoction of corn starch, food coloring, and water. The Jumpstart volunteers ask the children to feel the starch and see how dry and powdery it is. They put drops of food coloring in the water and talk about how at first it colors only some of the water, and then spreads throughout and colors the rest. The volunteer asks what would happen if they put in too much water,

Children learn words for things when they have fascinating experiences to talk about.

and then they do and find out how gooey the mix becomes. Then the volunteer asks what will happen if they add more starch, and they do and see the mix get drier and drier. At last the "Magic Mud" is ready. The children can mold it into shapes to make balls, animals, and people. The Jumpstart volunteer talks with them the whole time, asking what it is about to become, what it was before, what it might become.

So much language is used in this experience! The children practice very specific naming words and action words, and respond to and generate sentences in the present, future, past, and conditional tenses.

Use a Flannel Board

A flannel board is a flat surface on an easel on which you can stick cut-out shapes of flannel. Flannel boards are great devices for focusing children's attention during circle time, and for working with individual children.

A **weather report** (Charner and Murphy, 2002) can be done on a flannel board, for example. Cut out the shapes of a boy and a girl from pieces of flannel. Also cut out shapes for the sun, dark rain clouds, or snow flakes. Cut out articles of clothing—a hat and scarf, a bathing suit, an umbrella. Put the boy and girl figure on the flannel. Invite a child to give a weather report. Is it sunny outside? Is it raining? Is it cold? They can put the weather-related items on the flannel board, and also dress the boy and girl appropriately. Be sure to ask them questions and invite them to talk as they do the weather report. Remember that doing the weather report as a regular routine will make the vocabulary more familiar to the children.

Stimulate Story Talk

Stories provide natural ways to string words together, create excitement, and make language memorable. There are many ways to encourage story talk.

Retell a Favorite Storybook   Read the child *Frog and Toad* or *Henry and Mudge* or *Rosie's Walk*. Later in the day, read the story a second time, and a third. When the child has grown familiar with the story, invite her to retell the story as she pages through the pictures. Don't be surprised if she simply names the pictures first. In time, she will weave together more and more of a story (Sulzby, 1985).

Use Wordless Picture Books   Picture books are available that have very expressive pictures and no text. These invite children to make up their own stories to accompany the pictures. It can help for you to begin to narrate a story for a child so he gets the idea, and then let him finish the story—and narrate it the whole way through the next time. Some good bets are:

Mollie Bang (1996), *The Grey Lady and the Strawberry Snatcher*

Tomie de Paola (1981), *The Hunter and the Animals*

Mercer Mayer (1967), *A Boy, a Dog, and a Frog*

Mercer Mayer and Mariana Mayer (1975), *One Frog Too Many*

Brinton Turkle (1976), *Deep in the Forest*

You need not be limited to wordless picture books, though. Three- and four-year-old children can happily page through regular picture books and make up their own texts for them.

Use Flannel Board Props   Flannel board characters can accompany poems, chants, or stories. For example, when reading *Brown Bear, Brown Bear, What Do You See?* by Bill Martin, Jr., cut out animals from pieces of flannel: a brown bear, a yellow duck, a white horse, a grey wolf, and so on. Give each child a cut-out animal. Have the children join you as you repeat each verse. When the child's animal is called out, have that child attach the animal to the flannel board.

When retelling a story such as "Goldilocks and the Three Bears," cut out three bowls, chairs, and beds of different sizes; three bears; and a little girl. Tell the story of Goldilocks, posting up the shapes at the appropriate times. After you have told the story to the children two times, invite a child to retell the story, posting up the props as he does so.

Use Costumes   Simple strongly plotted stories such as "The Three Billy Goats Gruff" are fun for children to act out, and their acting is enhanced by the use of costumes. A furry shawl and a piece of Styrofoam cut and colored like a club can serve as the costume for the troll. Sets of horns made from cone-shaped paper can serve as costumes for the goats. The teacher or tutor can serve as the narrator at first, while the children recite the memorable parts:

Goat: "Trip, trap, trip trap, trip trap."

Troll: "Who's that walking across my bridge?"

Goat: "It is I, little Billy Goat Gruff."

Stimulate Imaginative Play

Imaginative play is a special domain of early childhood. It is a laboratory of the imagination, of images, and of language. While many children need little encouragement to initiate imaginative play, others appreciate the teacher or tutor's setting the stage.

Dorothy Singer and Jerome Singer at Yale University (1977 and 2001) have mapped out the territory of imaginative play. Their suggestions for activities all stimulate language development, although they move well beyond. Here are some activities they recommend.

Making Faces Since displays of emotions make up a portion of most imaginative play, we can teach children to be aware of facial expressions, their meanings, and the words that name them to help the children become aware of their own emotions and those of others. You will need a mirror, some pictures of facial expressions (you can cut them out of magazines), and some picture books in which emotions are conveyed. Begin by telling the child, "Watch me make a happy face" (then smile broadly). "Can you make a happy face?" Critique her efforts. "Yes! You're curling up the edges of your mouth." Let them see themselves in the mirror making faces. "Watch yourself making a happy face." (Hold the mirror in front of the child.) Practice with other expressions: angry, sad, excited, disgusted, and frightened. Show the children pictures of people showing emotional expressions and get them to name them. You can read children books about happy, sad, and excited people, and ask them to name the feelings.

Hats! Keeping a basket of hats around is a sure-fire trigger to fantasy play. A baseball hat, a fireman's hat, a nurse's hat, a sailor hat, a surgeon's cap, a chef's hat—each of these suggests a script for imaginative play. Have a child put on a fireman's hat and say,

"Hey, do you smell smoke? Yes! There's a fire in the building. Everybody make fire truck sounds! Pull on the hoses. They're heavy aren't they? Tell us how they feel. Now spray the water. Now, everybody make spraying sounds! How does the water look? Is there enough water? Now the fire is going out. Everybody make hissing sounds! Hooray! The fire is out! Everybody congratulate the fireman!"

Do the same for the other hats, and for others we haven't listed here.

Restaurant   A number of simulations can be arranged for groups of children. One is a restaurant scene. This activity, which is done in groups, includes the cook or chef, the patrons, and the waiter or waitress. Simple props help, like pots and pans for the chef, and a pad and pencil for the waiter or waitress. Other simulations can be: **riding on the bus**, an **airplane ride**, a **trip to the doctor**, a **classroom scene**, or a **safari to Africa to watch exotic animals**.

Scripted Fantasy Play   There are a few books like Michael Rosen's *We're Going on a Bear Hunt,* Pat Hutchins' *Rosie's Walk* (1971), and Mem Fox's *Hattie and the Fox* that script a fantasy by themselves. Children can chant

Kay Nozzolio
Preschool Teacher—Geneva Lakefront Center

Imagination

I particularly enjoy working with young children. They display a joy in learning and love to experiment. It is great to see this in their faces. As these children begin to develop and grow, I notice how their imagination grows. Through dramatic play and communicating with their friends, I really notice how they are beginning to progress. The children are using their words more and building on their vocabulary to express their thoughts and opinions. If they don't like something, they will tell you.

along with Rosen's narrator, complete with hand motions, as they cross streams, and work their way through tall grass. Mem Fox's *Hattie and the Fox* has a repeated verse that children find endearing. Children can take turns acting out all of the animals.

Finger Plays

Finger plays are a big category of activities that involve language, gestures with fingers and other parts of the body, and sometimes singing. Some, like the familiar "Eentsie Weentsie Spider" are done by making finger gestures as the song is sung. Others, like "John Brown's Ford" use whole body gestures. Either way, they are a very engaging way to involve children in rhymes.

"John Brown's Ford"   Folk singer John McCutcheon taught us this gesture song, which is popular with young children. The verse is sung to the tune of "The Battle Hymn of the Republic."

> **John Brown's** (Stroke your chin, indicating a beard)
>
> **Ford** (Turn an imaginary steering wheel with both hands)
>
> **Hit a bump** (Smack the palm of one hand with the palm of the other)
>
> **Upon the road** (Move your hand along in front of you, palm down);
>
> **John Brown's** (Stroke your chin, indicating a beard)
>
> **Ford** (Turn an imaginary steering wheel with both hands)
>
> **Hit a bump** (Smack the palm of one hand across the palm of the other)
>
> **Upon the road** (Move your hand along in front of you, palm down)
>
> **John Brown's** (Stroke your chin, indicating a beard)
>
> **Ford** (Turn an imaginary steering wheel with both hands)
>
> **Hit a bump** (Smack the palm of one hand across the palm of the other)
>
> **Upon the road** (Move your hand in front of you, palm down)
>
> **But he went rocking right along** (Rock back and forth in your seat).

The second time through, don't sing "John Brown's _____" but just stroke your chin instead of saying "Ford." The third time don't sing "John Brown's . . ." or "Ford" but do both gestures. Keep dropping out words until the whole song is done in mime.

Taste   The following poem is recited by the teacher or the tutors numerous times until the children learn it. Then they recite it, complete with finger gestures.

My ears can hear the baby cry	(Cup ear, as if listening)
My nose can smell the bacon fry	(Touch nose)
My tongue can taste the toast and jelly	(Point to your mouth)
My hands can feel my happy belly	(Lightly rub your belly)
My eyes can see my Mama smile	(Put hands on both sides of your eyes)
Because she looooves to feed this child	(Fold arms, smile, and rock)
And every day goes mighty well—	(Throw your arms wide)
'Cause I see, hear, touch, taste, and smell.	(Point to your eyes, ears, fingers, tongue, and nose)

Making Children Aware of Words and Sounds

As we said in Chapter Three, children who have an easy time learning to read in kindergarten and first grade are often those who are aware of the words they speak and hear and of the sounds in them (National Reading Panel, 2000). As a tutor in a preschool, you can teach word and sound awareness and help a child learn to read, even though reading happens a year or two after your time with her is done.

Word Awareness   Children who become readers need to be aware of words. When they focus on words as units of print, they need to find it natural to think of words in speech.

Magic Words   Say a word, like "hotdog." Then tell your child or children that you are about to tell a story that will have the word "hotdog" in it. They should clap their hands when they hear the word. Then start making up the story:

> "Last summer I went down to the park. I was really hungry, so I walked up to the food counter and ordered a—hamburger. The waitress said 'We don't have hamburgers. I'll have to make you a *hotdog*.'"

Later, you can ask a child to give you the magic word, and then you make up a story that has that word in it (After Hohmann, 2002).

Mary Hohmann suggests raising the challenge of the magic word game by asking children to listen for two words together. If those words are "ironing board," for instance, you might say,

> "My father was ironing his shirt. He was ironing it on the table, but the table got too hot. He was ironing it on the floor, but the floor was too dirty. 'Daddy,' I said. 'I know. Why don't you try ironing your shirt on the *ironing board*?'"

You can also have children listen for one word repeated two times, such as "Short short." They should raise their hands when they hear it.

> "There was a girl named Short. But Short wasn't short. Short was tall. Her friend Gladys was short. One day Gladys asked Short, "'If you were *short, Short*, your name would match you better.'"

Clap Out Words   You can make clapping games that are simple to elaborate. Clapping their hands to the words you pronounce is an easy way. Clapping in a sequence adds more challenge: hands together, hands on knees, hands on chest, hands on sides of thighs. Have children clap as you say words with emphasis:

> "When—I—go—to—Lu's—big—house
> I—like—to—play—with—Lu's—pet—mouse."

Listening to Rhymes   Listening to rhymes in words helps children learn to read (Bradley and Bryant, 1985). That is true for many reasons. First, it is an easy way to call children's attention to sounds in words and start to develop their **phonological awareness** (see Chapter Two). Second, because so many English words are built out of combinations of the same **onsets and rimes** (again, see Chapter Two), a child who is aware of rhymes in words has a terrific device for eventually reading a great many words. Here is what we mean. English has a reasonably small set of spelling patterns that are repeated to make many words. These spelling patterns are what linguists call **rimes**, and they are matched with different beginning consonants or **onsets** to produce many words. Some of them are:

-ack	-and	-ide
-ick	-ard	-oat
-ill	-ump	-up
-all	-ight	-ing

If a child can hear the rhymes in **sight** and **fight**, and **bit** and **fit**, and **tell** and **bell**, and **band** and **hand**, the day will soon come when he will be able to read **sight** because he already knows how to read **fight** and he is able to substitute the /s/ sound for the /f/ sound and read **sight**.

Songs, Chants, and Poems   Songs and chants are a natural way to get children to pay attention to rhymes—and also to memorize words, phrases, and sentences that will aid language development. Songs, chants, and poems are also a lot of fun to learn and repeat.

A song like this one invites hand claps and close attention to the rhymes:

Miss Mary Mack
Dressed in black
Silver buckles
Up and down her back

The lyrics are available in book form. Tutors and new teachers are advised to seek out collections of songs, especially those with tapes. The following are good bets:

Joanna Cole (1990). *Miss Mary Mack.* New York: Morrow.

Pamela Conn Beall, Susan Hagen Nipp, Nancy Spence Klein (2002). *Wee sing 25th anniversary celebration.* New York: Price Stern Sloan.

Dan Fox (1987). *Go in and out the window.* New York: Henry Holt.

Ella Jenkins (1997). *Ella Jenkins songbook for children.* New York: Music Sales Corp.

Kathleen Krull (1995). *Gonna sing my head off.* New York: Knopf.

Gerard Milnes (1999). *Granny, will your dog bite?* Little Rock, AR: August House.

Jose-Luis Orozco (1994). De colores and other Latin American folk songs for children. New York: Dutton.

———. (1997). Diez deditos and other play rhymes and action songs from Latin America. New York: Puffin.

———. (2002). Fiestas: A year of Latin American songs of celebration.

Ruth Crawford Seeger (1993). *American folksongs for children.* New York: Linnet Books.

All of these would be valuable additions to a tutor's or a teacher's personal collection.

Experienced teachers know many other songs that you can learn. Songs for transitions, songs that introduce tasks, songs to celebrate special people—all of these are essential; for a teacher's repertoire, as they contribute not only to children's development of language, but also to music appreciation and even to civilized classroom management. Write them down! And also, bring a small tape recorder so you can capture the tunes.

How will you lead the singing? You have three choices. You can

- Sing *a capella* (that means without any musical accompaniment),
- Sing along with a tape or CD, or
- Play an instrument to accompany the singing.

The latter is our preference. A guitar works just fine, and three or four chords and a capo (the device that changes your playing to another key) will get you through most songs. An even easier option is an autoharp. Playing an autoharp is as simple as finding a button for the desired chord, and pushing it down as you strum the strings. Children will appreciate the effort you make to bring live music into class.

Nursery and Jump Rope Rhymes   Spend part of every day reading rhymes to children. Rhyming materials come in many forms. The Mother Goose rhyme collections contain scores of them:

> *Peas porridge hot.*
> *Peas porridge cold.*
> *Peas porridge in the pot*
> *Nine days old.*

Read the rhymes to the children and ask them which words sound alike. Later, you can introduce the concept of **rhymes**—use the word: **rhymes**—and ask children to find the words that rhyme.

Rhyme Cube   After the children have learned at least six rhymes by heart you can prepare a **rhyme cube** (Charner and Murphy, 2002), a cube-shaped box with a picture taped on each side indicating a well-known rhyme. At circle time, one child is chosen to come forward, turn the cube to the picture of a rhyme she knows, and recite it for the group.

Other Sources of Rhymes   Rhyming books are other good sources of rhymes. Ludwig Bemmelmans' *Madeleine* books have long been popular. Look, too, for Roy Gerrard's *Rosie and the Rustlers* and other rhyming books; Charles Temple's *Train* and *Cadillac* and other titles; as well as Nancy Van Laan's *Possum Come a-Knockin'*. With all of these books, too, you can call children's attention to the words that rhyme.

Rhyming Games   A host of enjoyable games can be played with rhyming words. Looking around the classroom you can say, "I am looking at something that rhymes with **took**." And the children must say, "**Book**." Or you can say, "I am looking at a girl whose name rhymes with Dallas." And the children say, "Alice."

You can omit rhymes in a familiar poem and have children supply them:

> *Peter, Peter,*
> *Pumpkin _____.*

Children are asked to supply rhymes to complete couplets like:

> *Ding, dong, dell*
> *Kitty's in the _____ (well)*
> *Ding, dong, dasement*
> *Kitty's in the _____ (basement)*
> *Ding, dong, dimming pool*
> *Kitty's in the _____ (swimming pool)*

You can change a rhyme to a non-rhyming word and see if the children notice:

> *Fuzzy Wuzzy was a bear*
> *Fuzzy Wuzzy had no **honey**.*

You can supply a target word, such as "boy," and ask the children to raise their hands when they hear a word that rhymes with it, as you say a list of words: "Tea, tock, tack, *toy*." Or you can say a word like **bell**, and then pronounce the sound /s/; then the children say a new word that begins with the sound /s/ and rhymes with "bell": "sell."

Alliterations   Alliterations, common beginning sounds like "*Tom Tit Tot*" and "*Miss Mary Mack*" are another class of sounds that are worthy of attention.

We can read children books that practice alliteration. Especially fine for this use are Nancy Shaw's books:

Nancy Shaw (1988). *Sheep in a Jeep*. Boston: Houghton Mifflin.

Nancy Shaw (1992). *Sheep on a Ship*. Boston: Houghton Mifflin.

Nancy Shaw (1997). *Sheep in a Shop*. Boston: Houghton Mifflin.

We can repeat chants such as "Miss Mary Mack" and invite the children to watch our lips at we say the /m/ sound.

We can say a word that begins with a target sound and say, "I like words that start with the same sound as *peaches*. Raise your hand when you hear one: tambourine, sail, wig, *pack*, bell."

Exposing Children to Written Language

There are many ways to expose children to written language and to get them to use it. We can display print around the room. We can work print into children's play activities. We can set up activities that teach about print. And we can read to children.

Reading Aloud to Children

Reading aloud is one of the most useful things adults can do to nurture children's growth in literacy. Many of the abilities considered essential to literacy can be developed as children listen to a being book read aloud by a practiced adult. Among the main benefits of being read to are the following:

- *It expands their vocabulary.* As Stanovich (1992) has pointed out, there are words that are more commonly encountered in books—even children's books—than in conversation or from watching television. Listening to books being read aloud helps children learn a literate vocabulary.

- *It develops their ability to comprehend written language.* Reading comprehension is made of component skills that include perceiving main ideas and supporting details, making inferences, venturing predictions and confirming them, and visualizing in the "mind's eye" what is suggested by the words. Even young children can begin to develop these abilities from listening to a book read aloud and talking about it.

- *It gives the enthusiasm for literacy as they participate in the teacher's excitement.* When children are first learning to talk, parents slow down and exaggerate their speech and their gestures as if to say: "This is how language works. This is how we show excitement and interest. This is the way we soothe each other." Similarly, when adults read books aloud with expression, we have the opportunity to show children how written language conveys the full range of emotions. This will not only make literacy appealing to children, but also it will show them how to derive meaning and associate emotions with the language of print.

Reading aloud at least twenty minutes should be a regular feature of each day. You certainly don't need advanced training to read a book aloud successfully with children! Nonetheless, good preparation is rewarded by a

Alan Crawford
Emeritus Professor UCLA

Readalouds

Read aloud to children from big books with high-quality color illustrations. Read slowly, but naturally, pointing out key words from the written text in the story. Your job is to maintain comprehension, even if they don't speak English. They won't understand everything, but little by little, they will begin to recognize words of interest in English. Be sure to read books several times—then read them again in a week, again in three weeks, again in two months. What kinds of books? Try to find stories that are repetitive, predictable, and enjoyable.

more satisfying experience all around. First, we would recommend that you remind yourself of the benefits of reading aloud we described above. Second, we suggest following these steps when reading aloud to children.

Preparing the Book for Reading   Read the book through yourself before you read it to children. Decide if it is suitable for this group. Does it have enough excitement or depth to hold the interest of a whole group? If it is suitable, decide *how* you want to read it—with humor, with drama, with questions to whet curiosity? If there are voices to bring to life, decide how you want to make each one sound. If you decide to stop to ask for predictions or discussion, decide what the stopping places should be. If there are any words or ideas that will be unfamiliar to the children, make a note to pronounce them carefully and explain them to the children.

If the book has illustrations large enough for the children to see, practice reading the book through while you hold it in front and facing away from you, where the children will be able to read it.

Preparing the Children   Make sure the children are seated comfortably where they can see and hear you. Most teachers prefer to have the children sit on a carpet in front of them. Remind the children, if you need to, of the behavior you expect of good listeners: hands to themselves, eyes on the teacher, and ears for the story.

Beginning to Read   Show the children the cover of the book. Ask them what they know about the topic. If you want to arouse more curiosity, quickly show them some other pictures in the interior of the book (but not the last pages—keep the children in suspense about those). Ask them to make predictions about what will happen, or what they expect to find out in the book.

Turn to the title page. Read the author's name, and the illustrator's. Talk about what each one contributed to the book. It may help to point out that if only one name is given, then the illustrator and author are the same person. Otherwise, they should know that the author and illustrator both have important things to do to bring the book into being. (Publishers typically pay authors and illustrators equally, and usually encourage them to work independently of each other.) Remind the children of any other books they know by this author or this illustrator.

While Reading   As you read the book through the first time, ask for comments about what is going on. How is the character feeling? What is the character's problem? What do they think she can do to solve the problem? Ask the students to predict what will happen. Read a few pages, then stop again. Ask how things look for the character now. What is she doing to solve her problem? How is it working? What do they think will happen now? Why do they think so? Stop right before the end and ask for last predictions. (You can add to the suspense if you take an obvious quick look at the last page, but don't let them see it. Then ask the children to predict what will be on the last page.)

After the First Reading   Ask the children if the book turned out the way they thought it would. What made them think it would turn out that way, or why were they surprised? What did they like about the book? How did it make them feel? Why?

Rereading   Read the book a second time through. This time, you may want to take more time to look at the ways the illustrator pictured the action. Ask children to repeat any chants that are given in the book. If there is time, ask questions about characters and motives and other things you and the students find interesting about the book.

After Reading   Put the book on display in the library corner and encourage children to read it later during scheduled time in the reading center or between other activities. The children may especially enjoy taking turns reading it to each other.

Responding to Books

While children of all ages can talk about what they read (Martinez and Roser, 1991), younger children find it most natural to respond to books with their whole bodies: by getting up and moving around, by chanting chants, by acting out parts, and by drawing key scenes (Hickman, 1992). Bear in mind, too, that English learners have more opportunities to participate if meaningful responses to stories are encouraged through drama, music, and art, rather than through discussion only. English learners profit from repeating shorter chants, which become nuggets of remembered language, useful models of grammar and good for pronunciation practice.

Use Chants

An engaging form of response to a story is to repeat a key phrase or chant every time it occurs in a book. Children listening to Mem Fox's *Hattie and the Fox* love to repeat the animals' refrains: **"Good grief!" said the goose** (etc.). These books all have nice repeated phrases that children enjoy following along.

> Nadine Bernard Wescott (1990). *There's a Hole in the Bucket*. Philadelphia: Lippincott, Williams, & Wilkins.
>
> Simms Taback (2000). *Joseph Had a Little Overcoat*. New York: Viking.
>
> Simms Taback (1997). *There Was an Old Lady Who Swallowed a Fly*. New York: Viking.
>
> Cheryl Warren Maddox. *Shake It to the One That You Love the Best Play Songs and Lullabies Songbook*. Nashville: JTG of Nashville Audio.

Use Drama

Many children's books have clear patterns of actions that are easy for children to act out. Some books, like Michael Rosen's *We're Going on a Bear Hunt* (2003) and Frances Temple's *Tiger Soup* (1992) are already scripted for children to act out. Both have chants and movements that the children will enjoy.

The Three Billy Goats Gruff is not scripted as a play, but it has simple, repeated actions and chants that are easy for children to practice and perform. The whole story can be rehearsed and staged in half an hour. Single scenes of longer stories can be acted out, too, if time is short.

Acting is interpretation. Teachers can encourage children to interpret stories imaginatively as they rehearse the dramatizations: "How does the little goat feel when he sees the troll? Then how would he look? What would his voice sound like?"

Props help children get into character. In *The Three Billy Goats Gruff*, horns made of construction paper bring the goats to life, and a robe and a club add to the troll's fierceness. Construction paper masks tell us which character is Tiger and which one is Anansi the Spider in *Tiger Soup*.

Use Art

Drawing is a favorite way for children to respond to a story. The drawings may be extended by asking the children to leave space at the bottom of their papers, and to think of one line they want to dictate to the teacher as seen in the drawing. The children can rehearse reading these lines, and then take them home to read to family members.

The child drew the picture, then dictated the caption.

Dialogic Reading

The technique of **dialogic reading** is used when you are reading one-on-one with a child. It is a good way to introduce children to print, and also to help their language grow (Whitehurst and Lonigan, 2001). Dialogic reading helps put the child in the active role as a storyteller and not just as a listener. The activity is carefully structured to work with children's thought processes and expand their awareness, and also to be easy for a tutor to remember.

Two acronyms, PEER and CROWD, are used to remind us of the steps in Dialogic Reading.

The PEER technique is nicely suited to younger children. The acronym PEER stands for Prompt, Evaluate, Expand, and Repeat. The tutor proceeds by following these steps.

1. *Prompting* **the child to name objects in the book and talk about the story**. In other words, you might point to a picture and say, "What's that?" or "Hmmm. This looks interesting. What do you think that bear is doing?"

2. *Evaluating* **the child's responses and offering praise for adequate responses and alternatives for inadequate ones**. Now you listen to see if the child gives a fluent answer. Does she know the name for what's in the picture? Can she tell you a sentence about it? Or does she offer just a short phrase?

3. *Expanding* **on the child's statements with additional words**. This is a chance to "follow in order to lead," as we described above. If the child says "Dog!" now you are in a position to say, "Yeah, that's a cute cuddly dog, too. See his cute tail and his happy eyes?"

4. *Asking* **the child to** *repeat* **the expanded phrase or sentence**. Now you can say, "Can you say, 'That's a cute dog'?"

For more verbal children, you can use the CROWD technique. The acronym CROWD stands for the prompts or questions that ask for **Co**mpletion, **R**ecall, **O**pen-ended responses, **Wh**-prompts, and **D**istancing. Let's explain.

1. *Completion prompts.* **Here, the tutor leaves out a word or phrase for the child to supply**. For example, when you are reading Bill Martin, Jr.'s *Brown Bear, Brown Bear, What Do You See?* you might say "I see a yellow _____ looking at me."

2. *Recall prompts.* **Here the child is asked about things that occurred earlier in the book.** For example, after finishing the book you ask, "Do you remember some animals that Brown Bear saw?"

3. *Open-ended prompts.* **Here the child is asked to respond to the story in his own words.** For example, you might say "Now it's your turn: You tell me what is happening on this page."

4. *Wh- prompts.* **Here the adult asks** *what, where, who,* **and** *why* **questions.** For example, you might ask, "What is that yellow creature called?" Or "Who do you think Brown Bear will see next?"

5. *Distancing prompts.* **Here the child is asked to relate the content of the book to her life experiences.** For example, we might ask the child, "Do you remember when we saw a yellow duck like that one when we went on the field trip to the pond? Was it as big as this one?"

Arranging Classrooms for Literacy Learning

One obvious difference between homes that give a lot of support or a little support to young readers is the amount of print that is seen and used in them. A preschool setting can go a long way to make up some of those differences. The preschool room can show children both how print works and why it's important. It can also let children make sense of and create written language. Here are some ways that preschool rooms can immerse children in print.

Names   Even three-year-olds can easily find their names after some practice, so it's important to put their names on things that are theirs. Each child's cubby, of course, will have her or his name on it in big readable letters. Children's artwork will have their name on it, too, when it is displayed. In one preschool center, the tutors made a chart of the books the children peruse. Each time a child goes through a book, another star is place next to her name, which is written in big letters.

Labeled Objects   Objects around the classroom can have labels written in letters that are readable from far off. Every several days, the teacher and the children should take time together to "read the room" (Fountas and Pinnell, 1996) as the teacher or a student points to the labels with a pointer or ruler. The teacher reminds the students to listen for the first sound in

"Door" and notes that the first letter in "door" is D. Most children won't be able to read many of these words right off, but in time, they will read at least some of them. And it's instructive for them to see that things have names and that names can be written down.

Literacy Play   Props should be available to support children's dramatic play. Some of these props include reading and writing: the doctor's office has an eye-chart and a pad for the doctor to write prescriptions. The shelves in the grocery store center should have labels ("fruit," "soup," "bread" where the grocer should stock the items, and pads handy for the customers to use for writing grocery lists).

Classroom Post Office   The classroom should have a post office where children can mail letters. Each child can have a mailbox (constructed from 3'' cardboard tubes) for receiving mail. There is a big, cheerfully decorated mailbox for posting letters, which may be crafted of drawings, scribbles, and invented spellings. Children can be expected to write each other letters at least once a week; and the teacher can make sure she or he has written something to put in each child's box every few days.

A classroom post office in action.

Classroom Library   The classroom library is placed in a corner of the room. It has an adjacent carpet and bean bag chairs for flopping down on. There is space for displaying books so children can see their covers, and the books on display are changed every few days to catch the children's attention. Books cover a range of tastes, from informational books with bright illustrations to simple patterned books. Often the teacher reads a book or part of a book aloud and then places it on display in the library corner to entice children to look it over.

The classroom library includes books written by individual classroom authors, and books written or dictated by the whole class—books of favorite jokes and riddles, books about animals, books about the seasons.

Charts and Posters   Posters of children's books and pictures of authors, solicited from children's book publishers, are displayed on the walls. The children know Rosemary Wells and Dr. Seuss and Arnold Lobel and Cynthia Rylant and Alma Flor Ada, and they are excited when the teacher announces that she has a new book by one of them. There are charts of volcanoes, too, and maps of the town or neighborhood, with children's street names labeled. There are autobiographical posters hanging up with each child's name and something special that each child has dictated.

Writing Center   There is a writing center with paper, markers, and pencils. There are magazines that are sources of pictures that can be cut out, and glue to attach them as illustrations for the children's compositions.

All of these devices are passive ways of supporting literacy in the classroom. Now let us look at some active means.

The Language-Experience Approach

In order to learn to read and write, children need to know what reading and writing are. And here's the answer: Writing is talk written down, and reading is writing turned back into talk. We record our thoughts in the medium of print, and later—sometimes much later—we and others can bring it back into talk.

The **language-experience approach** (Stauffer, 1970) gives us a means to demonstrate these facts very clearly to children. You can use this method with a single child or with a group of up to a dozen children. If you are working with a single child, you write in printed letters half an inch tall. If you work with a group, you write on chart paper, and print in letters 1½ to 2 inches tall. Be sure to leave lots of space on the page for the children to illustrate the text.

Here is how the method works.

1. **Start with a stimulus.** The stimulus may be a field trip to the bakery, a banjo you bring to class, or an exciting story you read to the children.

2. **Talk about the stimulus.** The point is to get the children to attach words to the experiences, so your job is to get them talking, and also to interject some useful vocabulary into the conversation.

3. **Explain that you are going to write about the experience.** Together, you are going to choose your best words and write them on paper.

4. **Ask the children to give the writing a title.** What will they call the work? Write these words at the top of the sheet. This may be a good time to teach about letters and sounds, even if not everyone is thinking about such things. You can say "We're writing 'Fire Truck.' And look how I'm writing a letter F to make that sound /f/ /f/ /f/ for 'fire.'"

5. **Ask the children to tell you ideas to write down.** Remind them to speak slowly and clearly to help you write. If you have more than one child, ask each one to give you a sentence. Begin writing each child's sentence with "Takisha said . . ." This will help the child find her line later on.

6. **Read the text back to the children.** Read the text through once yourself, pointing to the words. Read it another time, **choral reading** this time, with the children reciting along with you as you point to the words. Read it a third time, this time **echo reading** the text; that is, you read a line, and then the children read the same line as you point to the words.

7. **Invite individual children to read parts of the text.** If you are reading the text with a group, ask a child to step forward, take the stylus, and read the words in a line. This is where it helps to have written the child's name by the line. "Takisha" is likely to read the words beside her own name.

8. **Have the children illustrate the text.** Adding an illustration to the text will help them remember what it was about later when they reread it.

9. **Post the text where children can see it, and reread it several times over the next few days.**

10. **With older children, make small copies of the text for them to illustrate, take home with them, and read to their family.**

Alan Crawford
Emeritus Professor UCLA

Conversation with Comprehensible Input

Talk to the children about things in their surroundings, about large-format color illustrations, anything of interest. Give them commands—"Put your finger on the dog in the picture." Ask simple questions—"How many ice cream cones do you see?" Accept responses in the form of gestures (e.g., pointing, holding up fingers); accept responses in the mother tongue (they understood the command or the question in English); accept one-word responses; and accept "errors" in their responses as signs of immaturity, not mistakes. Correction is a negative reinforcer in this situation. They will learn English as they learned their mother tongue.

Other Sources of Dictations

Dictated experience accounts have the advantage of recording children's own experiences in their own words—which is a source of excitement and motivation for many children (Ashton-Warner, 1963). But dictated accounts have the drawback of being disjointed and unpredictable, as might be expected of a text dictated by a group. Young readers like to read predictable and patterned text, and find such text easier to read. A compromise approach, then, is to have children learn a patterned text orally, then dictate that text to the teacher and proceed with the steps outlined above.

One source of patterned texts for dictation is songs and poems. Children can learn song verses, dictate them for the teacher to record, then sing them as the teacher points to the words. Children can make up their own verses to songs, too; and songs like "Down by the Bay" and "Corner Grocery Store" with their highly patterned verses are easy and inviting to innovate upon. Another source of patterned text is retold stories. After the children have heard a story read aloud to them a couple of times, they can retell a short and memorable version for the teacher to record and read back with them.

Morning Message and Planning the Daily Routine

A natural way to work writing into the day is to begin circle time by writing up the morning message or daily plan.

Morning Message   Morning message is a time for the teacher or tutors to discuss any special news, such as birthdays, expected visitors, the weather outside, the menu of the snack. After discussing each item, an adult will carefully write two or three words about that item on chart paper. It helps if the adult also draws a small symbol next to each item to help children identify it. The children read the words along with the tutor as the tutor points to them.

Daily Routine   With the daily routine, the teacher or team of tutors prepares a chart with boxes for the different activities children may choose to carry out. These are identified by symbols. For instance, book-making will have a book, art will have a paintbrush, dramatic play will have a mask. The teacher may discuss each option, invite children to choose what they will do, and then write each child's name in the box of her choice. The tutor reads back over the names, pointing to each one, and invites the children to read along.

Teaching the Alphabet

Children pay closer attention to the letters of the alphabet after they have come to notice writing as a holistic display (Gibson and Levin, 1975). That means children will spend considerable time doing pretend-reading of books and producing scribbles and mock writing before they come to focus consistently on individual letters. Nonetheless, teachers can help along their learning process by pointing out individual letters and by making displays of letters prominent in the classroom. And we should. If teachers hold off teaching children letters of the alphabet until children show "readiness" to learn, they may inadvertently penalize those children whose grandparents don't give them alphabet books and whose parents don't take them to the library. Children will undeniably learn the alphabet more quickly and easily when they have mock-read and scribbled their way to the point at which they are paying close attention to letters; but it is important to show all children the letters anyway, because this kind of learning is too important to delay.

Even as we invite children to write inventively, including mock writing, as we read to children and show them print, we also need to show them individual letters and demonstrate how they are formed. There are many ways of doing this.

- Alphabet letter cards can be posted around the room, with pictures of objects that feature that letter.

- Letter sorting and letter matching games can be arranged for children to play with at center time.

- Children can practice writing letters as the teacher writes a model. They may use large-ruled paper for this, or individual slates and chalk. Later, they may practice writing letters with a grease pencil on a transparency film overlaid on sample words with large letters.

- The alphabet song can be taught; and the teacher can point to the letter cards as the children sing the song slowly.

- Children's names can be written on cards and taped to wall, with the first letter of the first name written in a bright color.

- Plastic letters can be placed in centers to match with printed letters to form words.

- Sand paper letters on cards can be used in centers for children to trace with their fingers.

- Make alphabet books. The teacher prepares a blank book for the class and prints a letter on the top of each page, A through Z. The children think of objects that begin with the sound of that letter, and they take turns drawing pictures of those objects on the appropriate page.

Inviting Early Writing   The practice of writing can and should begin well before children know how to spell words or even to form letters. When children produce their own versions of writing and when they invent spellings, they are led into exploring how the writing system works, and are putting forth their own hypotheses about what writing looks like, how it is arranged on a page, how writing represents ideas, and how the spelling system works. As we have said earlier, the child who is actively investigating these questions is alert to the ways the system actually works. With encouragement and some lessons from the teacher, we expect to see that child progressing step by step and stage by stage to standard writing and spelling, and fluent and meaningful reading.

Early writing can be encouraged by teachers in several ways.

Captioning Drawings   One recommended way of encouraging writing is to have a child draw a picture and then write (or "mock write") a caption under it. Remind the children to leave space for this purpose, but keep a dark pen handy in case they forget!

Link Writings with Sounds   Have the children practice saying a sentence that practices alliteration, such as "Long-legged Larry lifts logs." Have the children draw a picture, and then write (or "mock write") a caption underneath. Some children will start to use the letter L in their mock writing, but probably not other sensible letters.

Incorporating Writing into Children's Play   We have already described ways of using writing in children's dramatic play. Sometimes as a tutor or teacher you will want to stress the writing aspect of the task. For instance, if you are pretending to take the child's order at a restaurant, you can recommend that he try the potatoes—and then as you write down his choice, remind the child that "potatoes" starts with the /p/ sound and show him that this sound is written with the letter P.

Involving Families in Emergent Literacy

The families of emergent readers can be involved in their children's literacy instruction in several ways. They can support their children's learning at home; work in concert with preschool teachers and tutors; or come into the classroom and take part in their children's learning activities.

Building a Relationship with Families

Preschool teachers and tutors learn to make good use of the natural points of contact they have with parents, especially those moments when parents drop off or pick up their children, or come to an open house.

The Jumpstart program for preschool children tries hard to involve families in their children's learning. Corps members—these are college students who volunteer as language and literacy tutors in local preschools—are urged to get to know the tutored children's families, and to work together with them to support the children's learning.

Jumpstart training teaches the Corps members to seize every opportunity to get to know parents, to put parents at ease with the preschool, and ultimately tomake them partners in their children's learning. Jumpstart suggests the following practices for tutors:

- Make themselves available to talk to parents when they drop off and pick up their children at school.

- Begin every conversation by saying a good thing about the child.

- Tell "one-sentence stories," which are brief anecdotes about what the child has been doing in the class. For example, "Michael makes up new rhymes when we sing songs in circle time." (Jumpstart Education and Training Team, 2003, p. 140)

- Ask parents about the child's life outside of the classroom: favorite books, toys, games, friends, and other activities. Knowing this information helps the tutor make the child feel more at home in the classroom and provides topics for conversation between the tutor and the child.

Danielle Marshall
Mid-Atlantic Program Manager, Jumpstart

Importance of Families

The greatest impact that I can see Jumpstart having on communities starts with the families of the children we serve. At present we encourage and provide frequent opportunities for families to become involved in their children's education via Jumpstart. My hopes are that this may eventually lead to better relationships between families and educational institutions overall. Schools are often a great place for families to learn about new and existing resources in the community. By increasing family involvement in education systems, many more of these resources can be accessed and shared throughout the community.

Reaching Out to Parents at Home

As part of their family literacy initiatives, tutors can send home to parents materials and ideas for helping develop their children's literacy. Four good examples of home-directed family literacy initiatives are *home books, book baggies, journals,* and *activity suggestions.*

Home Books   Simple books with very short and predictable texts can be written and sent home for children to read aloud to their parents. Eight-page home books can be made from one sheet of paper, printed on both sides, and assembled with the two double pages stapled one inside the other. Pictures are added to remind the children of what the text says. A sample text for a home book is shown in Figure 4.1.

Figure 4.1   A Sample Home Book

Where is my cat?	In the yard?
No.	In the closet?
No.	In the kitchen?
No!	He is under my bed!

The teacher reads the book through twice with the children before they take it home so they will be able to read it on their own. Instructions go home with the book for parents to read it with the child, and to encourage him to read the book many times. Home books can go home once a week. They provide useful practice in reading, and help children acquire concepts about print and even sight words.

Book Baggies   A book baggie consists of a simple paperback book in a bag with an activity sheet (such as instructions to draw a favorite character, a word hunt, an alphabet matching game) and perhaps a recording of the book on tape. Parents are encouraged to read the book with the child and take time to do the accompanying activity. Children should be told how to take care of the book bags when they go home. A book bag may spend several days at a time with each child, then be re-packed with new activity sheets and circulated to a different child.

Journals   A very helpful feature of the Jumpstart program is the journal that Jumpstart Corps Members send home to their children's families.

Involving Parents at School

When parents come into the classroom, they can help move instruction forward by reading to children, taking dictation, and helping publish and bind books. They can also tell stories, especially family stories, and they can demonstrate family traditions and crafts. In this way, they can make their families' lives part of the curriculum. In short, involving parents in the classroom not only provides an extra set of hands, but also it helps parents see the

Catherine Dowd-Reilly
Jumpstart Corps Member—Geneva, NY
"Reading to children develops their vocabulary, lays the foundations for pre-writing and pre-literacy skills, and introduces the magical world of books to children. Books introduce new characters, new ideas, and are food for the imagination."

importance of their children's learning and enables them to pick up techniques to help their children.

Some parents may be more willing than others to come into the class and participate. Parents of children who have been through Head Start may well have been involved in classroom activities already, and may have been trained to conduct activities such as reading aloud. For other parents, special invitations and special orientations will probably be required. The National Center for Family Literacy has developed a program to recruit and orient parents to help out in classrooms. A description of the program, called PACT for Parents and Children Together, can be found on the Center's website at www.famlit.org.

More Help in Family Literacy

A parent who was a regular volunteer in a Head Start classroom worried aloud because her child was going into kindergarten the next fall. "What's the problem? You can still volunteer in the kindergarten," the Head Start teacher pointed out. "Me? Suppose they hand me one of those school books to read?"

Like this mother, there are parents who do not volunteer to help in school and do not read to their children because they cannot read well themselves. For those parents, the agencies that used to provide adult literacy services are now offering family literacy programs, in which parents who are English learners are taught basic English and parents who need help with reading are taught to read to their children. These programs can be quite successful, since the imperative of helping her child can serve as a motivation for a parent to improve her own literacy skills, and the stories she practices to read to her child may be appropriate fare for her to develop her own reading fluency.

For information on programs that offer literacy services to parents, contact:

- Pro Literacy Worldwide (formerly Literacy Volunteers of America) http://www.proliteracy.org/
- The Barbara Bush Literacy Foundation at www.barbarabushfoundation. com
- The National Center for Family Literacy at www.famlit.org
- The Even Start program at www.evenstart.org.

Putting It All Together: Emergent Literacy in the Preschool

Let's say you've just volunteered to help out in a preschool room as a language and literacy tutor. You've read the previous pages, and learned a huge amount about children's language and literacy and how they develop. You have amassed a good repertoire of strategies that you can use. But the night before you go into the classroom for the first time, you're wondering: "Where do I begin? And what do I do after that?"

Jumpstart is a successful movement that places thousands of volunteer college students in preschool settings (Jumpstart, 2003). Jumpstart tutors are assigned one-on-one to a child in a three-year-old or four-year-old classroom. They work with their children in two-hour blocks, twice a week. They divide their time into three kinds of activities:

1. **One-on-One Reading Time** (10–20 minutes). Here the tutor reads a book with the child and talks about it. Note that one-on-one reading may occupy as little as five minutes a day at the beginning of the year, but as the relationship between the child and the tutor develops, and as the child's confidence grows, it can expand to 20 minutes at a time, or even more. In Jumpstart, tutors use the dialogic reading approach described earlier in this chapter, and with younger children, they use the PEER strategy (Prompt-Evaluate-Expand-Repeat). They try to match books with the children's interests, and they are careful to:

- Introduce words into the discussion to build the children's vocabulary.

- Point to parts of the book (the cover, the title, the author's name, the way the print goes on the page, words that are repeated and that the child might begin to notice).

- Use rhymes and chants—leaving pauses for the child to fill with rhyming words and to say the repeated parts out loud.

Tutors are careful to prepare children to transition to the next activity.

2. **Circle Time** (10–15 minutes). During circle time, the children and their tutors gather for a common activity. Circle time is an opportunity for children to develop a sense of community with each other and to learn social skills. Circle time activities are a nice blend of teaching and play; they are

lively and interesting, but they also teach concepts and share language. Circle time activities usually include interactive songs, finger plays, and games—but they can also include a language-experience writing and reading activity.

3. **Choice Time** (60–90 minutes). The third and longest part of the Jumpstart session is subject to the children's choices. The children are given a set of options to choose among. These may be one-on-one activities with their tutor or a small group activity chosen from a prearranged set. Jumpstart, like other high-quality early childhood programs, carefully emphasizes the element of choice, and provides several strategies to support children's ability to choose for themselves.

Still, Choice Time is valuable time for children to develop language and learn about print, so tutors are careful to work in games that practice listening and talking, reading, writing, and learning about print as their options.

One-to-One Reading	*Circle Time*	*Choice Time*
Reading aloud to the child	Morning Message	Dramatic play
Dialogic reading	Daily routines	Working with letters
Talking about books	Songs	Practicing and performing a play
	Chants	Playing with letters
	Poems	Other small group games
	Language Experience Accounts	

Transitions

Young children engage in tasks more fully and easily when they have a sense of control and when they have time to adjust to new activities. Changes in activities should be few, and well thought out. Children should be told ahead of time that there will be a change to a new activity. Many teachers sing special songs like this one (to the tune of "The Farmer in the Dell"):

It's time to eat a snack,
It's time to eat a snack.
Go wash your hands and then sit down.
It's time to eat a snack.

Other Time Arrangements

If you are volunteering to tutor children in a preschool setting, you may opt to spend different amounts of time in the room. You might arrange your time as follows:

1. **One-on-one reading** (20 minutes). Reading through and talking about two or three books, possibly using the dialogic reading procedure.

2. **Presentation and discussion of a stimulus** (10 minutes) (a live bunny rabbit, a picture of a trip you took, etc.) and a discussion, using the "Following in Order to Lead" or the "Science Talk" procedure.

3. **Game time or other activity** (30 minutes). This might involve drawing or dictated writing about the stimulus or dramatic play, or playing with words, rhymes, or letters.

chapter five

What Now?

Perhaps you are not tutoring a child right now, but feel ready to do it. Let's talk about your situation first. Later in this chapter we will talk about pathways from tutoring into teaching. But first let's talk about tutoring.

Suppose You Want to Tutor?

We believe that tutoring is more fun and more productive if you do it through an organized program. You get an orientation to the tasks of teaching and working with children, and also, arrangements of the places and

times are already made for you to get together with the child you are tutoring. Someone is usually available to observe your work and give you point-
ers. And there are others to share the excitement of the work and learn from.
It is a sad fact of contemporary life that schools are necessarily so security-
conscious that they may not be able to accept your offer of help unless you
make connection through an organized program. Even then, you should expect to abide by whatever security arrangements the schools ask of you.

School-based Tutoring Projects

Many preschools and elementary schools have their own well-organized volunteer tutoring programs. You can check online and see if they have a web
page that explains their program, and if not, call them directly.

College- and University-based Tutoring Programs

Service-Learning is now a common feature of higher education. Ever since
Jonathan Kozol's book *Illiterate America* (1988) set out a vision of college
students serving their communities as literacy tutors, tutoring projects have
proliferated. In the 1980s, the Student Literacy Corps promoted tutoring
activities on hundreds of campuses. This was followed in the 1990s by the
"America Reads Challenge," which made the important breakthrough of
allowing students who are eligible for work-study funds to use their time
tutoring. This practice is now widespread on college campuses.

In response to America Reads, several excellent guides to tutoring
young children (usually grades 1–4) have come on the scene. Two of the
best of these are Johnston, et al.'s *Book Buddies* (1998) and Darrell Morris'
Howard Street Tutoring Manual (1999). Both books give detailed guidance
to tutors. *Book Buddies* devotes attention to how you would organize a tutoring project on your campus, as well as to the care and feeding of tutors.
Both books were written with the assumption that the tutors would work
under the supervision of an experienced teacher or literacy coach.

Jumpstart

An up-and-coming tutoring program on college campuses is Jumpstart.
This program recruits, trains, and fields college-age tutors to work with preschool children, with the aim of improving the children's school readiness.

From its beginnings at Yale University, in the past decade, the program has grown to serve 6,000 children in 44 communities, and to involve the participation of 1,600 students from 50 campuses across the United States. Like tutors in the America Reads projects, Jumpstart students, too, are eligible for work-study support. Graduates of Jumpstart are eligible to apply for Pearson Teacher Fellowships, to ease the transition into professional work as an early childhood educator. For more information about joining Jumpstart, or in establishing a new Jumpstart chapter on your campus, you can contact the organization through their web-page: http://www.jstart.org/about/.

From Tutoring to "A Life"

Now that you know how much of a difference you can make in children's lives—and in the lives of the adults, family members, and citizens they will soon become—we want to close this book by asking you a suggestion. Why don't you keep helping children learn to read?

To the Reader This chapter will tell you what you need to know if you decide that you like knowing that you have something really valuable to offer and you like knowing that some kids are trusting you to help them grow. We won't put the hard sell on you. But we hope this book has made it clear how much this country needs not only volunteers, but also full-time professionals to commit themselves to helping children learn to read and write. This chapter will tell you what to do next if you want to look into teaching as a job option. Please share this information with other people whom you think might be interested.

Every idea we have related in this book has come from people like you. People who accepted an invitation during their college years, often a random invitation, to work with young people, and then decided that's what they wanted to keep doing. Jason Long began as a tutor in college, then went on to become a preschool teacher. Ana Pujol became an elementary teacher after volunteering in America Reads in College. So did Mike Harms.

Lauren Buchmann, senior at Hobart and William Smith College, is an Americorps NCCC (National Civilian Community Corps) alum. She also spent two years at HWS serving as a mentor for young children in low-income areas of Geneva, New York. Now she is a Jumpstart team leader for eight college corps members working with eight preschoolers.

Jenna Logue worked as an America Reads tutor in college, then stayed on at her school to manage the tutoring programs for others. (Jenna is going off to Harvard next year to pursue a career in education.)

Alan Farstrup tutored children in college, went to Afghanistan to teach as a Peace Corps Volunteer, continued teaching back in the United States, became a college professor, and is now the executive director of the International Reading Association, the world's largest literacy organization.

Darrell Morris went to the mountains of West Virginia as a VISTA volunteer (Now Americorps), came back to Virginia to teach, set up a storefront tutoring center in Chicago, and now does research on how children learn to read and helps set up volunteer tutoring programs in many parts of the country.

Aurora Martinez, the executive editor of this book, was a teacher of English as a Second Language before she began publishing literacy materials for a large educational publisher. So was Kathy Smith, the copyeditor.

Darrell Morris
Professor of Education Appalachian State University
**Designer of *Early Steps* early literacy program
and *The Howard Street Tutoring Manual***

My interest in literacy development was sparked by my VISTA service in a poor western Kentucky community in the early 1970s. There, I routinely saw bright-eyed, curious six-year-olds fail to learn to read in first grade because they lacked basic, prerequisite experience with written language. The situation affected me deeply and led me to question my nation's commitment to an equal start for all children. I have since learned in my career as a reading educator that well-supervised volunteer tutors can make a huge difference in the literacy development of young children (pre-school through second grade). By reading and discussing stories with youngsters, by listening to them read, and by helping them with letter sounds, committed tutors can provide at-risk children with a "life line" to literacy. In the process, the tutors themselves will experience a great reward: watching a young child learn to read.

Suppose You Decide You Want to Teach?

Early Childhood Education

If you decide you want to work with three- or four-year-old children, in many communities you can do so without earning a teaching certificate. However, we hope this book has demonstrated that there is much to be learned about children's development of cognition, sociality, language, and literacy. There are teacher certification programs in most states that prepare you to teach early childhood education (from a few weeks old through kindergarten, or up through grade two, in most states). Some programs specialize in early childhood special education, and others specialize in family literacy. All are fascinating areas of study and service.

Pearson Teacher Fellowships

For those who have served as Jumpstart Corps Members, Pearson Publishing supports the Pearson Teacher Fellowships. These fellowships are intended to smooth your way into a professional career as an early childhood educator. Fellows enjoy significant financial, training, and other support through the program. Benefits include:

- $12,500 stipend over two school years, to supplement your preschool teaching salary;
- Mentoring from a Pearson professional;
- Increased early childhood education knowledge and teaching experience through an intensive eight-week Summer Training Program, including a full-time teaching practicum as an assistant teacher;
- Job-search assistance, including résumé revision and interviewing skills training;
- Direct service with children who need your help the most;
- Ongoing professional development resources and opportunities.

Also, because Fellows work in centers serving children and families from low-income communities, they may qualify for partial or full cancellation of Federal Perkins and/or Stafford college loans.

Tanya Chretien
First Year Fellow, teaching in Boston

I decided to join the PTF [Pearson Teacher Fellowship program] because of several factors.

I love children, and spent four years in college preparing to be an early childhood educator. I also welcome a challenge. But during senior year, I began to wonder if teaching in a public school was right for me, or if I would be better off somewhere else. I wanted to work in a place where I could use my knowledge and love of children. I wanted to work in an environment where there was some flexibility and everything was not centered around the MCAS [Massachusetts Comprehensive Assessment System] test. Enter the idea of Head Start and other early childhood classrooms.

I really liked the ideas and values I learned in Jumpstart through my experiences as a corps member and a team leader. Though I had several non-Jumpstart experiences and internships throughout college, the values that I learned in Jumpstart served as my guide, and helped to shape my philosophy about education. I was (and still am) excited about my Jumpstart experiences coming full circle. I remembered how it felt to be a corps member and I was excited to work with the current corps members. I knew that through the Pearson Teacher Fellowship I would have a chance to work with students who had some similar values as I did because of Jumpstart.

Suppose You Decide to Teach in the Public Schools?

There is a critical need for talented teachers at all levels in the public schools. You should realize that teaching in public schools requires that you earn a professional teaching certificate. Earning a certificate means that you will need to take courses in child development, the teaching of reading, and related subjects. Usually, you will need to have a supervised student teaching experience. These courses and the student teaching experiences are well worth the time. As we have said, there are things you should know about children's learning processes that you can gain from courses. And there is a world of procedural knowledge about teaching that you can gain from student teaching. Even if you have had a rewarding experience as a tutor, planning and teaching a whole class of children day after day is a whole different level of challenge—and you will be grateful for the chance to learn the craft from an experienced teacher.

You can read about the teaching certification requirements for each of the fifty states by going onto the website of each state's department of education:

Alaska	http://www.eed.state.ak.us/
Alabama	http://www.alsde.edu/html/home.asp
Arizona	http://www.ade.state.az.us/
Arkansas	http://arkedu.state.ar.us/
California	http://www.cde.ca.gov/
Colorado	http://www.cde.state.co.us/
Connecticut	http://www.state.ct.us/sde/
Delaware	http://www.doe.state.de.us/
District of Columbia	http://www.k12.dc.us/dcps/home.html
Florida	http://www.fldoe.org/Default.asp?bhcp=1
Georgia	http://www.doe.k12.ga.us/
Hawaii	http://doe.k12.hi.us/
Idaho	http://www.sde.state.id.us/Dept/
Illinois	http://www.isbe.state.il.us/
Indiana	http://www.doe.state.in.us/
Iowa	http://www.state.ia.us/educate/
Kansas	http://www.ksbe.state.ks.us/Welcome.html
Kentucky	http://www.education.ky.gov/
Louisiana	http://www.doe.state.la.us/lde/index.html
Maine	http://www.state.me.us/education/
Maryland	http://www.marylandpublicschools.org/MSDE
Massachusetts	http://www.doe.mass.edu/
Michigan	http://www.michigan.gov/mde
Minnesota	http://www.educationminnesota.org/
Mississippi	http://www.mde.k12.ms.us/
Missouri	http://www.dhe.mo.gov/

Montana	http://www.opi.state.mt.us/
Nebraska	http://www.nde.state.ne.us/
Nevada	http://www.doe.nv.gov/
New Hampshire	http://www.ed.state.nh.us/
New Jersey	http://www.state.nj.us/education/
New Mexico	http://www.sde.state.nm.us/div/fin/trans/
New York	http://www.nysed.gov/
North Carolina	http://www.dpi.state.nc.us/
North Dakota	http://www.dpi.state.nd.us/
Ohio	http://www.ode.state.oh.us/
Oklahoma	http://www.sde.state.ok.us/home/defaultie.html
Oregon	http://www.ode.state.or.us/
Pennsylvania	http://www.pde.state.pa.us/
Rhode Island	http://www.ridoe.net/
South Carolina	http://www.sde.state.sc.us/
South Dakota	http://www.state.sd.us/deca/
Tennessee	http://www.state.tn.us/education/
Texas	http://www.tea.state.tx.us/
Utah	http://www.usoe.k12.ut.us/
Vermont	http://www.state.vt.us/educ/
Virginia	http://www.pen.k12.va.us/
Washington	http://www.k12.wa.us/
West Virginia	http://wvde.state.wv.us/
Wisconsin	http://www.dpi.state.wi.us/
Wyoming	http://www.k12.wy.us/index.asp

Alternative Routes to Teaching

Many states offer alternative programs to make it easier to begin teaching. In Arkansas, for example, students with a 2.5 grade point average can begin teaching right away, and work toward certification with weekend workshop and summer programs. The state of Florida has an elaborate system to enable not-yet-certified teachers make a quick transition into the classroom (see Figure 5.1).

Figure 5.1   Florida's Alternative Pathway to Teaching

Florida's Alternative Certification Program includes the following components for implementation by Florida school districts:

- **Survival Training** to ensure an initial period of preparation before the teacher assumes responsibility for the classroom
- **CD-ROM** to train users on features of the web-based learning management system used to deliver the learning activities
- **Support Team** to coordinate and support the professional development of the teacher
- **Peer Mentor** to offer face-to-face feedback and assistance throughout the learning experience
- **On-line Tutor** to provide guidance, feedback, and assessment of work products developed through the program's learning activities
- **Building Level Administrator** to verify successful demonstration of all education competencies
- **Outside Educator** to offer feedback as a collaborative partner from higher education or a district level supervisor
- **On-line Professional Preparation Learning Activities** to provide in-depth, in-time acquisition of the Florida Educator Accomplished Practices
  - Assessment
  - Communication
  - Continuous Improvement
  - Critical Thinking
  - Diversity
  - Ethics
  - Human Development & Learning
  - Knowledge of Subject Matter
  - Learning Environments
  - Planning
  - Role of the Teacher
  - Technology
- Opportunities for supporting roles by **Collaborative Partners** to assist school district implementation
- **Pre-Assessment** to determine the learning needs of each teacher
- **Individual Action Plan** to outline the structured learning experiences for each teacher
- **On-line Professional Preparation Learning Activities** to provide in-depth, in-time learning experiences for acquisition of professional education competencies

(continued)

Figure 5.1   Continued

- **Summative Assessment Tasks** to ensure a standards-based method of determining mastery of the professional education competencies
- **Database Tracking System** to document the progress of each teacher in successfully demonstrating the Florida Educator Accomplished Practices
- **Professional Education Test** to demonstrate knowledge of educational pedagogy.

Developed to incorporate findings from research literature on effective alternative certification programs, best practices in distance learning, and a legally defensible standards-driven assessment system, Florida's Alternative Certification Program embraces continual quality improvement. Its implementation demonstrates that learning is engaging, meaningful, and on-going. That is an educationally sound message for learners of all ages.

Teaching in Cities

Many American cities have incentive programs to help college graduates get into teaching.

New York City Teaching Fellows: http://www.nycteachingfellows.org/. New York City has 5,000 fellowships available to college graduates who will teach and earn a master's degree at the *same time*.

Teach New York: http://www.nycenet.edu/teachnyc/default.htm. Teach New York is a teacher recruiting effort aimed at college students and career changers.

Teach DC: http://www.teachdc.org. Washington DC offers this incentive program to attract teachers.

Check out these city school web pages to find pathways into teaching.

San Antonio Public schools	http://www.saisd.net/ADMIN/Personnel/index.shtm
Chicago Public Schools	http://www.cps-humanresources.org/Careers/career_index.asp?bhcp=1#
Houston Public Schools	http://www.houstonisd.org/HISD/portal/jobs/front/0,2746,20856_2556,00.html

El Paso Public Schools	http://www.episd.org/Employment/
St. Louis	http://www.slps.org/SLPS_Update/career_opportunity/career.htm
Los Angeles	http://www.lausd.k12.ca.us/welcome.html
Atlanta	http://www.atlanta.k12.ga.us/careers/teach_aps1.html
Boston	http://www.boston.k12.ma.us/jobs/
Albuquerque	http://ww2.aps.edu/
New Orleans	http://www.nops.k12.la.us/District/careers.html
Seattle	http://www.seattleschools.org/area/employment/index.dxml
Kansas City	http://www.kckps.org/#emp
Philadelphia	http://www.philsch.k12.pa.us/offices/recruitment/

Getting a Master's Degree

Some states—New York and California are two—require master's degrees to continue teaching beyond a few years. Even those states that don't require master's degrees offer higher salaries to teachers who have them. Because the courses required for teacher certification can approach the number of courses needed for a master's degree anyway, if you have a bachelor's degree or are close to earning one by the time you decide to teach, it will be worthwhile to earn certification and get a master's degree at the same time.

If you do get a master's degree and you aren't already certified to teach, you might look for an MAT program: Master of Arts in Teaching. These programs give you the courses you will need for certification, plus a term of student teaching, and maybe even a couple of liberal arts courses. You can complete an MAT program before you begin to teach.

If you are able to get a teaching job on a temporary basis without being certified, many states will let you count a year of teaching experience as if it were student teaching, especially if the school arranges for you to have a mentor. In that case, you will take your graduate courses in the evenings and during the summer. Most schools that offer master's degrees in education schedule their courses in the late afternoon or evening, after public schools close. Unless you come across a program that offers courses in the daytime, you may as well plan to teach and earn your master's degree after hours.

Teach for America

Teach for America deserves special mention. It's an initiative that recruits talented college graduates and sends them for a two-year stay in urban and rural sites around the United States. Candidates may teach Mexican American children in the Rio Grande Valley, Navajo children on a reservation in New Mexico, in the cities of New York or Washington, in rural North Carolina, or in a number of other sites (see Figure 5.2). You don't need to be certified to join Teach for America. The program has links with local colleges and universities and will help you get the courses and experience you need in order to become a licensed teacher. By the way, although teaching licenses are issued by individual states, they are usually recognized in other states. Or nearly recognized. If you are certified in one state, you may have to take a local examination or even an extra course to be certified in a new state.

Figure 5.2 Teach for America Sites

References

Children's Books

Bang, M. (1996). *The grey lady and the strawberry snatcher.* New York: Alladin.

De Paola, T. (1981). *The hunter and the animals.* New York: Holiday House.

Fox, M. (1992). *Hattie and the fox.* Chicago: Scott, Foresmann.

Hutchins, P. (1971). *Rosie's walk.* Chicago: Scott, Foresmann.

Martin, B. Jr. (1996). *Brown bear, brown bear, what do you see?* Illustrated by E. Carle. San Diego: Henry Holt.

Mayer, M. (1967). *A boy, a dog, and a frog.* New York: Dial.

Mayer, M., and M. Mayer (1975). *One frog too many.* New York: Puffin.

Rosen. (1989). *We're going on a bear hunt.* New York: Margaret K. McElderry.

Turkle, B. (1976). *Deep in the forest.* New York: Puffin.

Professional References

Aitchison, J. (1998). *The articulate mammal.* New York: Routledge.

Bauman, K. J. (2001). *Home schooling in the United States: Trends and characteristics.* Working Paper Series No. 53. Washington DC: Population Division, U.S. Census Bureau.

Beck, I., M. McKeown, and L. Kucan. (1999). *Bringing words to life.* New York: Guilford Press.

Berliner, D. C., B. J. Biddle, and J. Bell. (1996). *The manufactured crisis: Myth, fraud, and the attack on America's public schools* (Rev. ed.). Boulder, CO: Perseus Publishing.

Bredekamp, S., and C. Copple. *Developmentally appropriate practice in early childhood programs* (NAEYC Series #234.) Washington, DC: National Association for the Education of Young Children, 1997.

Chomsky, N. (1975). *Reflections on language.* New York: Pantheon.

Clay. M. M (1975). *What did I write?* Portsmouth, NH: Heinemann.

Clay, M. M. (1993). *Reading Recovery: A guidebook for teachers in training.* Portsmouth, NH: Heinemann.

Clay, M. M. (2000). *Concepts about print: What have children learned about the way we print language?* Portsmouth, NH: Heinemann.

Delpit, L. (1996). *Other people's children: Cultural conflict in the classroom.* New York: New Press.

DeVillers, J., and P. DeVilliers (1975). *A first language*. Cambridge, MA: Harvard University Press.

Ehri, L. C. (1989). The development of spelling knowledge and its role in reading acquisition and reading disability. *Journal of Learning Disabilities* 22(6): 356–365.

Erikson, E. (1993). *Childhood and society*. New York: Norton.

Finders, M., and C. Lewis. (1994). Why some parents don't come to school. *Educational Leadership* 5(8): 50–54.

Grissmer, D. W., A. E. Flanagan, J. H. Kawata, and S. Williamson. (2000). *Improving student achievement: What state NAEP test scores tell us*. Santa Monica, CA: RAND.

Halliday, M. A. K. (1975). *Learning how to mean*. London: Edward Arnold.

Hart, B., and T. Risley. (1995). *Meaningful differences in the everyday experience of young American children*. Baltimore: Brookes.

Hart, B., and T. Risley. (1995). *The social world of children learning to talk*. Baltimore: Brookes.

Heath, S. B. (1982). What no bedtime story means: Narrative skills at home and school. *Language in Society*, II, 49–76.

Heath, S. B. (1983). *Ways with words*. Cambridge, England: Cambridge University Press.

Hoff, E. (2001). *Language development*. New York: Wadsworth.

Hohmann, M. (2002). *Fee, fie, phonemic awareness*. Ypsilanti, MI: Highscope Press.

Hymes, D. (1972). Models of the interaction of language and social life. In J. Gumperz and D. Hymes (Eds.), *Directions in sociolinguistics: The ethnography of communication* (pp. 35–71). New York: Holt, Rinehart, and Winston.

Johnston, F., M. Invernizzi, and C. Juel. (1998). *Book buddies*. New York: Guilford.

Juel, C. (1994). *Learning to read in one elementary school*. New York: Springer Verlag.

Jumpstart Education and Training Team. (2003). *Jumpstarting school success: A toolkit for corps members*. Boston: Pearson Custom Publishing.

Kozol, J. (1988). *Illiterate America*. New York: Plume.

Luxembourg Income Study. (2000). http://www.lisproject.org/.

Morgan. K. Personal communication, June 15, 2004.

Morris, R. D. (1999). *The Howard Street tutoring manual: Teaching at-risk readers in the primary grades*. New York: Guilford.

Morris, R. D., and R. Slavin. (2002). *Every child reading*. Boston: Allyn and Bacon.

National Assessment of Educational Progress. (1994). Washington, DC: U.S Government Printing Office.

National Assessment of Educational Progress. (2003). Washington DC: US Government Printing Office.

National Center for Educational Statistics. (2003). *Parent involvement in children's education: Efforts by public elementary schools.* http://nces.ed.gov/surveys/frss/publications/98032/.

National Center for Educational Statitstics. *The National Adult Literacy Survey.* http://nces.ed.gov/naal/design/about92.asp 1992.

National Reading Panel. (2000). *Report of the National Reading Panel: Teaching children to read—an evidence-based assessment of the scientific research literature on reading and its implications for reading instruction* (SuDoc HE 20.3352:R 22). Washington, DC: U.S. Department of Health and Human Services.

Newport, E..L., H. Gleitman, and L. Gleitman. (1977). Mother, I'd rather do it myself: Some effects and non-effects of maternal speech style. In C. E. Snow and A. Ferguson (Eds.), *Talking to children: Language input and acquisition.* Cambridge, England: Cambridge University Press.

Orfield, G., J. Wald, and C. Sanni. (2001). *School segregation on the rise despite growing diversity among school-aged children.* Cambridge, MA: Harvard Graduate School of Education, 2001.

Orfield, G. J., and J. Yun. (June 1999). *Resegregation in American schools.* Cambridge, MA: The Civil Rights Project, Harvard University.

Piaget, J. (1926). *The language and thought of the child.* London: Routledge & Kegan Paul.

PISA. (2000). *The OECD program for international student assessment.* http://www.pisa.oecd.org/.

Read, C. (1975). *Children's categorization of speech sounds in English.* Urbana, IL: National Council of Teachers of English.

Richards, I. A. (1929). *Practical criticism.* New York: Harcourt, Brace.

Schaffer, R. H. (2004). *Key concepts in developmental psychology.* New York Sage Publications.

Shaffer, R. H. (1977). *Mothering.* Cambridge, MA: Harvard University Press.

Singer, D. G. (1996). *A Piaget primer: How a child thinks.* New York: Plume.

Singer, D. G., and J. L. Singer (1977). *Partners in play.* New York: Harper and Row.

Singer, D. G., and J. L. Singer (2001). *Make-believe: Games and activities for imaginative play.* Washington: Maginative Press.

Skinner, B. F. (2002). *Beyond freedom and dignity.* Indianapolis, IN: Hackett Publishing Company (Originally Published in 1971).

Snow, C., M. S. Burns, and P. Griffin (Eds.). (1998). *Preventing reading difficulties in young children.* Washington: National Academy Press.

Stauffer, R. G. (1970). *The language experience approach to the teaching of reading*. New York: HarperCollins.

Stanovich, K. Are we overselling literacy? (1992). In C. Temple and P. Collins (Eds.). *Stories and Readers*. Norwood, MA: Christopher-Gordon.

Stanovich, K. E. (1986). Matthew effects in reading: Some consequences of individual differences in the acquisition of literacy. *Reading Research Quarterly* 21(4): 360–407.

Staveteig, S., and A. Wigton. (1999). *1999 snapshots of America's families II: Key findings by race and ethnicity*. Urban Institute. [http://www.urban.org/content/research/newfederalism/nsaf/snapshots/1999results/keyfindingsbyraceandethnicity/keyfindings.htm]

Stern, D. (2004). *The first relationship: Infant and mother*. Cambridge, MA: Harvard University Press.

Sulzby, E. (1985). Children's emergent reading of favorite storybooks: a developmental study. *Reading Research Quarterly 20*, 458–479.

Temple. C., R. Nathan, N. Burris, and F. Temple. (1993). *The beginnings of writing*. 3rd ed. Boston: Allyn and Bacon.

U.S. Department of Education. (1994). *Strong families, strong schools*. Washington, DC: U.S. Government Printing Office.

Vygotsky, L. S. (1986). *Thought and language*. Rev. Ed. Cambridge, MA: MIT Press.

Walsh, D., G. Price, and M. Gillingham. (1988). The critical but transitory importance of letter naming. *Reading Research Quarterly 23*(1), 108–122.

Watson, J. (1926/1998). *Behaviorism*. (Originally published in 1926).

Whitehurst, G. J., and C. Lonigan. (June 1998). Child development and emergent literacy. *Child Development 69*(3): 848–872.

Whitehurst, G. J., and C. J. Lonigan. (2001). Emergent literacy: Development from prereaders to readers. In S. B. Neuman and D. K. Dickinson (Eds.), *Handbook of early literacy research*. New York: Guilford Press.

Willms, J. D. (1999). *International adult literacy survey: Inequalities in literacy skills among youth in Canada and the United States*. Ottawa: Ministry of Industry.

Woodward, V., J. Harste, and C. Burke. (1984). *Language stories and literacy lessons*. Portsmouth, NH: Heinemann.

 **Index**